SOW
WHAT?

DISCIPLESHIP MADE REAL

JAN WHITMORE

WestBow Press books may be ordered through booksellers or by contacting:

WestBow Press
A Division of Thomas Nelson
1663 Liberty Drive
Bloomington, IN 47403
www.westbowpress.com
1-(866) 928-1240

ISBN: 978-1-4497-8633-5 (sc)
ISBN: 978-1-4497-8634-2 (hc)
ISBN: 978-1-4497-8632-8 (e)
Library of Congress Control Number: 2013903356

Printed in the United States of America.
WestBow Press rev. date: 3/21/2013

To Des, my devoted, gentle and loving husband – my lifelong friend – promoted to glory 4 April 2011.

His text messages always ended: "Hurry home!" For sure I am.

Table of Contents

Foreword (1)

What a delight to read Jan's new book, *Sow What*? Evie and I have come to know Jan well over the twenty-plus years of her ministry with Mission Encouragement Trust (MET), of which she is a co-founder. Her ministry has involved travelling thousands of miles through many nations to bring hope, peace, pastoral counsel, and encouragement to missionaries. She is an encourager, truly a "Barnabas", "a daughter of encouragement", even as Barnabas was "a son of encouragement".

Jan is a friend to many, including my wife, Evie, and me, and since 1995 has been a frequent participant in our Barnabas International conferences in the United States. As a diligent student of the Scriptures, she has shown her love and knowledge for the Word of God through faithful, passionate, and persistent teaching at seminars and retreats around the world. I have listened to her speak, and as I have read her discipleship materials I have discovered she carefully studies the Word. She spends much time in prayer, and only then does she speak and write.

God has used this book to stir my own heart. So often, while reading the book, I would say, "Listen to this, Evie. This is really good. Isn't that a good word?" I have read, studied and preached on the parable of the sower and have seen pastors encouraged because of it. They, like Jesus, are sowers of the seed. They too get various responses to their preaching, even as Jesus did. The same sower ... the same seed ... but results vary, depending on the soil. Jan has taken this and added rich personal insights into each of the four soil conditions and to what we must do to prepare good soil in our hearts to receive the seed.

As she wrote the book, she was richly moved and transformed. The

Holy Spirit, who inspired the Scriptures, illumined the Word to her. To quote her, she experienced a "spiritual tsunami". I too was blessed; I experienced a revival in my own heart. I pray that you will also be open to rediscovering the truth of this parable – the sower, the seed, and the soil. The book is written to stir your heart, and I am sure you will be enriched through reading and applying it to your life and ministry. In addition to personal benefit, the book is practical and urges the user to share its message in small groups – "life groups" – to encourage Christian discipleship and growth.

– Dr Lareau Lindquist, founder of Barnabas International, United States

Foreword (2)

Jan Whitmore, a gifted Bible teacher and encourager, has produced a book that will enable participants to help each other deepen the level of their Christian commitment. This is a practical book intended to be used by small groups of four or five people agreeing to work together over an eleven-week period or longer, if they so decide. Based on the parable of the sower, it invites participants to reflect on the nature of God, the sower, and the seed, which is His Word. If we allow this seed to fully impact our lives, it will produce in us a Christ-like character. As the parable makes clear, the way in which biblical truth takes root in us depends on our individual responses. These responses, as both the parable and Jan Whitmore's book remind us, vary considerably from person to person and are likened to different kinds of soil.

The second part of the book challenges members of each study group to reflect on how fully, or otherwise, they are allowing Jesus' teaching to shape their individual lives. All the chapters provide some informative material to enable members to focus their thinking on the chosen issue and then end with a series of questions for group discussion, reflection, and prayer.

– Revd Dr Nigel Scotland, Tutor Trinity College, Bristol and honorary research fellow, The University of Gloucestershire, United Kingdom

Preface

If I place a seed in the palm of your hand and ask, "What kind of seed is it?", unless you are a very keen gardener, you would probably have to admit you don't really know. Some might look at me strangely and respond with the obvious, "It's a seed". How many would say specifically, "It's a cucumber seed" or "It's a pumpkin seed"? One seed can look just like another to the uneducated eye, and its value is unknown. A seed is so small and insignificant that you can be forgiven for not knowing what special treasure lies in the palm of your hand.

In fact, a seed is never "just" a seed; there is so much more to it than can be seen. Inside that seed lies hidden a dynamic and unique identity that has the power and will to become what it was destined to be. God made it that way. It may become a beautiful flower, full of colour and aroma, a laden fruit tree, or a nourishing vegetable. That one tiny seed was created with the ability not only to fulfil its own destiny, but to produce many seeds, securing future harvests. There is inexhaustible potential in one seed! However, let's not get carried away; staring quizzically at a seed in the palm of your hand will not prove its pedigree. The innate value of seed can only be realised when planted in soil.

Never is this more pertinent than when we come to understand the incredible identity and power of God's seed, His living Word. It is only when it is planted deep in the soil of our hearts that we discover its true creative and powerful nature. In the soil it renews our mind and steadily reveals its pedigree, purpose and ability to transform our lives.

This book invites you into a short discipleship season of seed-planting. It is a life course packed with challenge and insight, written to help you discover and experience the dynamic spiritual growth concealed within the DNA of one tiny yet efficacious "seed" – the Word of God.

Have you ever wondered why some believers are radically changed while others remain spiritually lacking and immature? Why do some get saved but never experience an ongoing transformation of heart? What hastens and what hinders growing strong in our faith? Is there a problem with the seed, or is there a problem with the soil? Jesus answers all those questions, and more, in the parable of the sower. It is time for some new and fresh insight from the Holy Spirit.

The layout of this book purposefully facilitates both individual study and in-depth fellowship. For the duration of the study (possibly eleven weeks, depending on the pace chosen), you are encouraged to form a "life group" of no more than four or five fellow believers who share your thirst and desire for greater intimacy with God. It is my hope and prayer that the groups will not only cross over the boundaries of denomination, mission, social standing, and culture, but will facilitate the forging of lasting, devoted friendships in the body of Christ.

In encouraging believers to meet in life groups for discipleship, I am not suggesting the displacement of the crucial function of church home groups. I believe both have a unique and valuable role. This discipleship material could be used successfully within a church home group, but larger groups may inhibit deeper sharing.

I experienced a 'spiritual tsunami' when the Holy Spirit began to teach me kingdom truth from the parable of the sower. It was a "rhema" (from the Greek: "utterance", or "thing said") word directly from God. The Holy Spirit acted as His agent to securely bed its life-changing truth into my thoughts, attitudes, and behaviour. Like the bright sun slowly rising along the horizon, truth rose to bless me with an accelerated surge of spiritual growth. It was not long before I noticed new spiritual shoots steadily pushing through the soil of my heart. After years of longing for inner transformation, I finally found the key to exchanging spiritual mediocrity for spiritual verve. Hour upon hour, as I studied this parable, my Bible sparkled into life.

It took me a while to realise that the Holy Spirit's disciplined and orderly method of teaching would mean committing to more than a quick skim of the Bible, flitting over passages like a butterfly. He had prepared a discipleship training programme aimed at assimilating kingdom truth into the fabric of my life. I was to *experience* the rich, life-changing realities of truth contained in this parable; the days of just "head knowledge" were well and truly over! I slowly moved from knowing I *could* be transformed to *being* transformed, and it wasn't without cost. I had to reckon with not only reprioritising and reordering my life to give time for God to plant His seed into my heart, I had to be prepared to face the reality of contaminated soil that hindered, and in some cases forbade, the growth I longed for. It was surely worth the high price to discover the sheer joy and liberty that accompanied purity of heart. My infectious excitement rubbed off on all with whom I fellowshipped, and now I offer to you some of what I have learned.

For twenty years I have had the great privilege of working alongside my colleague and friend Mintie Nel. In 1992 we founded Mission Encouragement Trust (UK Charity 1063403), a ministry of spiritual encouragement, care, and growth to international Christian missionaries. In the early years, as God's servants, we travelled in a campervan around Eastern Europe supporting the ever-expanding mission community who were relocating east, responding to the deprivation caused by a failed communistic era.

As we journeyed, we quickly discovered an acute sense of spiritual dryness in God's people. Many missionaries were stationed in isolated locations where fellowship and teaching were sparse. Over time, as their inner spiritual reserves dwindled against the growing demands of ministry, there were few opportunities for refilling and replenishing. Wanting to help forced us into waiting on the Lord; we were pressed to receive scriptural encouragement from the Lord and quickly learnt how to effectively pass it on. Short homilies, like the parable of the sower, soon developed into in-depth discipleship material.

Since 2001, having come to the end of our strength to travel thousands of miles on the road in our campervan, the Lord refocused our time, abilities and energy into hosting retreats for single missionaries in South

Africa, Eastern Europe, the United Kingdom, and the Middle East. Mission Encouragement Trust (MET) hired beautifully appointed retreat centres, and missionaries took a week away from their location of ministry to spend quality time with us and our gifted MET staff team. Participants needed time away from the unique pressures of ministry in geographical isolation to enjoy the fellowship of other singles. They fellowshipped both readily and easily, understanding one another without having to explain a lot! Having had the opportunity to offload, be heard and understood, they returned to the mission field for another season of fruitful service with new strength and courage. Many arrived at the retreats broken, disillusioned and ready to give up. Thankfully, many left restored and refreshed in the Lord. Through a programme of discipleship teaching, worship, meditation, small groups, prayer ministry, and recreational activities God poured out His delight and restorative joy.

Each retreat brimmed with love, acceptance, affirmation and excellence. Over a period of twelve years, 2001 – 2013, we have had the pleasure and privilege of receiving more than five hundred missionaries from more than forty different international mission agencies, at twenty-one retreats. It was a joy to raise financial sponsorship for each missionary to attend. God birthed a passion in our hearts to facilitate special times for His people to sit at the feet of Jesus—times of undivided and attentive listening, learning, and responding. We are still busy with that calling.

In writing *Sow What?,* the first of a discipleship series, I am joining hands with a groundswell of Christian believers who are excitedly rediscovering the primary mandate that Jesus gave to the Church—to *make* disciples. Jesus said in Matthew 28: 19–20: "Go therefore and *make* disciples of all the nations, baptizing them in the name of the Father and of the Son and of the Holy Spirit, teaching them to observe all things that I have commanded you; and lo, I am with you always, even to the end of the age" (NKJV, emphasis added). First of all we must be a disciple of Jesus and then we must *make* disciples. Disciples are made they don't just appear! Spiritual growth leading to godly maturity happens through intentional discipleship.

When I started out I was simply going to tidy up some of the discipleship materials I'd written over the years for various mission and church assignments. I had no intention of writing a book! However, as I once again engaged with the parable of the sower, I became deeply aware that my Bible notes of twenty years could be a help to other disciples of Jesus. I felt urged by the Holy Spirit to release them to a wider audience. I trust you will be blessed both as you study alone and when you gather with a few fellow disciples to share.

Acknowledgments

There are many friends to whom I owe so much. Writing a book is the summation of a lifetime. It has meant leaning heavily on the influence, example and training of mentors and trusted friends who share a common passion for discipleship and love for God's eternal Word.

I first pay tribute to Colin Springate, my Corps Cadet Guardian in the Gillingham Salvation Army, United Kingdom. It was Colin who first noticed this raw and reluctant recruit and began teaching me the Scriptures. Leading me into the baptism of the Holy Spirit in January 1975, his love for the Word ignited desire for truth in my heart.

I pay tribute to Joe and Judi Portale, international leaders of Youth With A Mission (YWAM), a world-wide mission which trains and equips young people to fulfil the Great Commission of Jesus. I was a student of the Crossroads Discipleship Training School (CDTS), Lausanne, Switzerland, in 1989, and the Leadership Training School (LTS), Kona, Hawaii, USA, in 1991, under Joe and Judi's excellent leadership. I woefully lacked confidence but they saw something in me, opening doors of opportunity that set my feet firmly on the path of realising YWAM's motto, "knowing God and making Him known". I have no doubt that my early growth and development, frequently through facing many weaknesses and failings, was at the expense of many patient and longsuffering YWAM team-mates. When you think you know it all it is far better for everyone that you quickly discover that you don't!

I delight to honour my mentor, spiritual teacher, intercessor and long-time friend, Lori Lee, in Atlanta, Georgia, USA. After thirty years, she is still alongside, giving wise advice and shaping my life. Her deep love for Jesus through the Word of God has certainly rubbed off on me. We have walked and grown together, step by step. She has been part of the team, together with Maritha Esterhuizen, Jeanne Cilliers, and Vickie Blair, that checked the manuscript's biblical content and highlighted the many typos, inaccurate grammar, and misuses of commas and semicolons, among many other things!

I also pay tribute to Pastors Reuven and Yanit Ross for their exemplary and inspirational example in disciple-making. Such dedication and passion for God and His Word is rarely seen. It has spurred me on to be like them! Friendship is a precious gift forged in the rigors of life. Reuven and Yanit are eternal friends.

Then there is Mintie Nel, who has been my fellow-worker and close friend for more than twenty years. We met at Youth With A Mission in Lausanne, Switzerland, in 1990. She is a living example of gentle tenaciousness as a disciple of Jesus Christ; she lives the life of an overcomer in the face of long-term chronic illness and acute pain in all her joints. She truly is a disciple of Jesus who intimately knows God and joyfully pays the price to make Him known to all who enquire. She never gives up, and has never once abandoned her assigned post as chief supporter, intercessor and loving friend in this writing project.

The spiritual battle to produce this book has been both immense and personally costly in terms of attacks on my health. I thank my USA Mamma Margie for her intercession and the many telephone calls and emails of biblical encouragement. She has urged me on! We share a close and precious partnership in the gospel.

Above all, "Thank You, Lord, and may Your name and Your name only be glorified".

Part I: The Seed

Introduction:

How Do We Begin?

Growth is the only evidence of life.

J. H. Newman

So, you want to grow? Be encouraged, because that sincere desire pleases the heart of our heavenly Father like no other. This week marks the beginning of an exciting and challenging discipleship season. This is a study that has the potential to transform your life if you are open to revelation by the Holy Spirit. For years you might have just skipped over the parable of the sower, but now the Holy Spirit wants to use it as His discipleship tool.

This is the first time you are with those who will share in your eleven-week journey of growth; therefore, it is fitting that as a discipleship group you begin by reading the introduction together. Take a few minutes to introduce yourselves, and then ask one person to read this introductory chapter aloud for all to enjoy.

Jesus, in His unique style of choosing everyday things to awaken spiritual understanding, spoke to the rural crowds about principles of farming. His story was simple, direct, and familiar. Farming itself was not hard for them to grasp, but it was understanding the parable in the light of the kingdom of God that was utterly lost on the majority. Most "missed it" and ironically, this parable is all about making sure you "get it". Jesus' teaching was life-changing for hearers who revealed a spiritual hunger for spiritual revelation, but for the majority, spiritual deafness and blindness kept them from its blessing. Sadly, it is much the same today, and we need to discover *why* as we study the parable of the sower.

This is much more than a personal study; it is a life-changing experience, written with the desire to see believers seriously and intentionally evaluate their own process of discipleship. Equally, it was written to encourage believers to share spiritual things, naturally and regularly, with discussion centred on the biblical study. What we learn on our own is confirmed and comes to life when we share it with others. I want to stimulate corporate discipleship, where it is not about "me" but what *God* is doing "in me and through me". Discipleship means belonging to one another and growing stronger together in Jesus. This level of fellowship adds fuel to kindling, creating a fire. I hope it will stimulate lively interaction and forge a deep mutual love and respect.

Believers meet for many reasons, such as eating, camping, cycling, walking, visiting a beautiful garden, or going to the theatre or a concert. All these activities are lovely and good, but we also need to rediscover the depth of joy and freedom that comes only when we intentionally invest time and money in mutually sharing the impact of God's living Word on our lives. This is not just occasionally discussing a passage of Scripture; it is wrestling deeply with truth to the point of inner transformation by the Holy Spirit. There are plenty of good Bible studies that appeal to our minds, but far less discipleship material that challenges our minds to be renewed and our hearts to change.

I have laid out this study in such a way that you first work on your own, reading and studying a chapter at a time. Then you meet with your chosen life group to discuss and share your answers to the questions that the study offers for your consideration.

- After the teaching section, each chapter closes with a "Selah Moment". *Selah* means "pause and think about that". It is commonly used in the Psalms. In this book, a Selah Moment includes prayer and some probing questions to consider and answer. You will think about these on your own, and I suggest you carefully journal your thoughts. You will need a notebook in which to write down insights, thoughts, feelings, questions, and anything new the Holy Spirit gives you.

- Each chapter ends with a suggested outline for your next life group meeting and a Scripture for meditation.

Forming a Life Group

I am passionate about small, committed discipleship groups that meet together *in a structured and purposeful way* to facilitate an exciting environment for spiritual growth. Every opportunity you take to share what God has been teaching will accelerate your own spiritual development. The life group must commit to systematically following the study and meeting on a regular basis. The frequency of meetings should be decided on by the group members. Some groups may want to meet weekly for an eleven-week discipleship season; others may prefer meeting every two weeks, extending the discipleship season to twenty-two weeks. The use of the material can be flexible as long as *all* members of the life group are in agreement.

It will be beneficial for the life group to do the following today:

- decide what the purpose of the group is;
- hear individuals express their expectations for the group; and
- hear how individuals would like to use the materials.

This initial meeting should iron out questions such as, who leads, how to best study, and how often and where to meet. Make it clear at the beginning that the life group is not centred on eating and drinking. By all means, enjoy tea, coffee, or a cold drink and a plate of cookies, but keep it simple. The focus of the life group is fellowship around the discipleship study, not food. At the end of the season of growing together, you may want to share a special meal during which you reflect on the time spent together and how it impacted your life.

- Don't make the group any larger than *four or five people*. A larger group inhibits sharing at a deeper level. If the group is larger, meet in two or three separate groups within the same location. At the end of the session, the groups can come back together to share the joy of what has been experienced.
- Each member should commit to making the life group a priority for the duration of the course. Partial attendance does not work well. A bond of love, honour, respect, and understanding will be established when *all* fulfil what has been agreed upon. The opposite is also true: group spirit will languish when some participate half-heartedly, displaying indifference to the life group time. When members have more important commitments at exactly the time of your life group, it devalues the commitment made and dishonours fellow group members. So whatever agreement you make, all should stick to it! Obviously there are genuine reasons for non-attendance, such as sickness or an emergency, but agree to let the group know. Where possible, the meeting time can be changed. Our purpose is to cut out the lame excuses! Satan specialises in lame excuses, which birth apathy and indifference. These times of meeting and sharing will become precious, building meaningful relationships that last.
- Plan ahead. Diarise your meetings, each no longer than two-and–a-half hours. This gives fifteen minutes for everyone to arrive and settle and fifteen minutes at the end to enjoy some simple refreshments. Two hours should be guarded for sharing aspects of the discipleship study and praying.
- Try to meet where the telephone can be silenced, and have group members switch off their mobile phones. Don't just put them on silent with vibration; switch them off. This is hallowed time

together. In this way, you honour the Lord and the people you are with. Normally there is nothing that cannot wait two-and-a-half hours!

- Many of the life group questions are quite penetrating and personal. It is crucial that the group understands and abides by *confidentiality*. Nothing shared should be mentioned outside the group unless you have the person's permission.
- When sharing, try not to use spiritual clichés; use everyday language. Allow group members to share without interruption. Learn to listen to others and not be wholly consumed with what you want to say. As you listen to others, pray for them. It is not easy to make yourself vulnerable at this level, but the rewards of a closer and richer fellowship are immense.
- After uninterrupted sharing has finished, take some time to exchange questions and give feedback. Debate was a normal and healthy part of the life of disciples in Jesus' day and an essential way to learn. However, we must learn in debate to disagree respectfully and without tantrum or offence. Remember, we are co-disciples – we are all learners.
- Many meetings will conclude with confession in prayer. Allow time for each one to pray. When the Holy Spirit starts to touch hearts, revealing weaknesses and failures, it can become emotional. People feel vulnerable and exposed, and there may be weeping. Please allow your fellow group members to weep and mourn their sin without any intervention. At this stage, don't halt their repentance. Be empathetic, supportive, and merciful, but give space.
- When praying for each other, keep prayers centred on what was shared. Don't drift into other topics. Be honest with one another when this happens. Use this opportunity to pick up on some of the

desires that each has shared and express them to the Lord. Make sure everyone in the group receives prayer. If you run out of time, the next time you meet start with those who haven't been prayed for.

This is your first meeting as a life group, and everyone is bound to be a little nervous, not knowing what to expect. The idea in life group is to have a safe and secure place where you can be honest with God, yourself, and group members. Being open and honest is where growth begins. So please, resist answering the following questions in the way you think you *should* answer them or in a way that will particularly impress others. Let's be done with impressing!

- What has been your *most enjoyable* experience with a garden?
- What has been your *most frustrating* experience with a garden?

Our hearts are God's garden, and our heavenly Father is the gardener.

- What do you think is God's most enjoyable experience in the garden of *your* heart?
- What do think frustrates Him in the garden of *your* heart?

Let's pray: ask one person to *close in prayer.* Before you leave, nominate someone to purchase *a packet of seeds* for the next life group.

Scripture for Meditation

'Those who sow in tears shall reap in joy. He who continually goes forth weeping, bearing seed for sowing, shall doubtless come again with rejoicing, bringing his sheaves with him' (Psalm 126: 5–6 NKJV).

Chapter 1:

A Mystery or a Message?

Seeing and Hearing, Perceiving and Understanding

Ask yourself three questions:

1. How deep is my understanding of God's Word?
2. How much truth is able to penetrate deeply into my heart?
3. Is the Word of God a mystery or has it become a life-changing message?

Read Mark 4: 1–29. Do not be tempted to skip this step.

We are going to concentrate on the following verses: "And He said to them, 'To you it has been given to know the mystery of the kingdom of God; but *to those who are outside,* all things come in parables, so that "*Seeing they may see and not perceive, and hearing they may hear and not understand lest they should turn, and their sins be forgiven them*"'. And He said to them, 'Do you not understand this parable? How then will you understand all the parables?'" (Mark 4: 11–13, NKJV, emphasis added).

Two Couplets

Referencing Isaiah 6: 9, Jesus uses two interesting couplets: "seeing and not perceiving", and "hearing and not understanding". It would be helpful to mark them.

When the Holy Spirit takes "seeing" to a deeper level we can "perceive" spiritual things that previously we were blinded to. When the Holy Spirit awakens our "hearing" He gives spiritual "understanding" that previously was not known naturally. It is the Holy Spirit that brings revelation to our hearts and only He can unlock the mysteries of God to our understanding. If we desire to have more understanding we need to ask the Holy Spirit!

1 Corinthians 2: 9–10 says, "But as it is written: "Eye has not seen, nor ear heard, nor have entered into the heart of man the things which God has prepared for those who love Him." But God has revealed them to us through His Spirit. For the Spirit searches all things, yes, the deep things of God" (NKJV).

Only "seeing" and "hearing", without any perception or understanding from the Holy Spirit, means we will only have natural and shallow comprehension—our faith can only be superficial. We may have "seen" and "heard" a lot of truth, but sadly, we are unmoved and remain unchanged; we are devoid of sensitivity to God's holiness and our sin. Therefore, we do not make any move toward God in humble repentance that leads to transformation. We may be able to quote a lot of Scripture that we have memorised, but there is no spiritual awakening. We may believe in God but it has not altered our lives. Life goes on as it did before! God's Word is unproductive in our hearts, and we have little understanding of what the kingdom of God is all about.

It is impossible to understand the mystery of the kingdom of God by our natural mind. The parable of the sower teaches us that the hardened condition of our heart is the problem, forbidding access to God's Word. Our hearing profits little and we blindly miss the point. We live our life "on the outside" of truth (Mark 4: 11) displaying only a respectable veneer of spirituality. What God communicates remains a *mystery*.

However, when "seeing and hearing" is accompanied by Holy Spirit "perception and understanding", everything God communicates is a life-giving *message*. The Word is alive in our spirit by the Holy Spirit! We hear with eager sensitivity to God's voice, engaging and readily responding to what we have heard. The Holy Spirit has access to our surrendered hearts, we are obedient to God's truth, and we are actively being transformed into the likeness of Jesus. We are devoted and true disciples of Jesus, listening and applying truth to our lives.

God Communicates with Us

Father, Son, and Holy Spirit long that believers not only see and hear, but perceive and understand the kingdom message. They long to take us deeper into their confidence! God does not want us ignorant concerning who He is, His immense love, His ways, His plans and redemption. He desires for our spirit to be connected to His Spirit, with all channels open to His voice.

We are created by God with five *natural* senses. They are our receptors: sight, smell, hearing, touch, and taste. Through them we naturally understand the messages of our environment. When we were born-again of the Spirit of God our *spiritual* senses were sensitised. We gained spiritual sight (insight), spiritual smell (discernment), spiritual hearing (perception), spiritual touch (anointing of the Holy Spirit), and spiritual taste (hunger and thirst for righteousness). They became our spiritual receptors to spiritual truth, inspired and orchestrated by the Holy Spirit. He communicates with us by a dynamic combination of all five and we gain a deeper understanding and insight into things of the kingdom of God. Psalm 36: 9 puts it this way: "For with You is the fountain of life; in Your light we see light" (NKJV). Under the Holy Spirit's tutelage, what might have begun as a puzzling *mystery* is unveiled as a dynamic and divine *message*.

The Bible references all five senses:

1. Matthew 5: 8: "Blessed are the pure in heart for they shall *see* God" (NKJV, emphasis added).

2. Philippians 4: 18: "Indeed I have all and abound, I am full, having received from Epaphroditus the things sent from you, a *sweet-smelling* aroma, an acceptable sacrifice well pleasing to God" (NKJV, emphasis added).

3. Deuteronomy 4: 36: "Out of heaven He let you *hear* His voice, that He might instruct you" (NKJV, emphasis added).

4. Matthew 9: 21: 'If only I may *touch* His garment, I shall be made well" (NKJV, emphasis added).

5. Psalm 34: 8: "O *taste* and see that the LORD is good; blessed is the man who trusts in Him!" (NKJV, emphasis added).

According to the Encarta dictionary, we reach the deeper level of understanding and perception by a process of using the five senses to acquire information about the surrounding environment or situation. In the context of our parable, those who not only *see and hear,* but also *perceive and understand,* are awakened by their spiritual senses at every level of their being to supernatural revelation from God. They personally *experience* the power of the message. They can *see* the farmer sowing, *smell* the field, *hear* the sharp whoosh as another handful of seed is broadcast on the ground, *touch* the harvest, and *taste* the bread, discerning things that escape the notice of most people.

Our spiritual senses are sharpened by exercise in God's Word. Hebrews 5: 12–14 says, "For though by this time you ought to be teachers, you need someone to teach you again the first principles of the oracles of God; and you have come to need milk not solid food. For everyone who partakes only of milk is unskilled in the word of righteousness, for he is a babe. But solid food belongs to those who are of a full age, that is, those *who by reason of use* (of the oracles of God) have *their senses exercised* to discern both good and evil" (NKJV, emphasis added). God wants us to have mature spiritual discernment.

Blurred Vision

Since age three, I've regularly had to have my eyes checked. Without glasses objects appear blurred and misty. A visit to the optician is a blessing; I leave with lenses that give me 20/20 vision. The process of assessment is interesting. The optician asks various questions and then positions a rather ugly and uncomfortable frame on my nose. One by one he places corrective lenses into the available slots within the frame. I am asked to evaluate whether "one" is better than "two", or if "three" is better than "four". In this manner, he builds up a personal prescription. I don't understand the technicalities of the process, but I love that special moment when, finally, the right lenses are inserted and all the letters on the wall are suddenly clear.

I recently went to the optician to collect new glasses. Meticulous in checking that everything was okay, the optician asked me to read as far down on the reading chart as I could. Naturally, with a new prescription all the lettering was sharp and clear. I contentedly slipped the glasses off my nose for a minor frame adjustment. Immediately, without glasses, the chart became a total blur! One minute I could read the finest print and the next, without corrective lenses, I could not make out one word. I smiled as I considered remonstrating that the print on the card must be flawed – after all, perhaps there was no need to pay the small fortune for new glasses! However, as adept as I am at blaming, it would have been ridiculous to blame the reading chart, for the problem was entirely my eyesight. I sensed the Holy Spirit's delight as I grasped a simple revelation.

When it comes to the mystery of God's Word, we all stand on level and ignorant ground. We may be able to make out shapes, or guess the meaning of what we think we have heard, but our natural senses are utterly blurred, darkened and flawed by sin. Humility acknowledges two things: we are totally "in the dark" and He is utterly "in the light". It is only "in His light" that "we see light". It is only the Holy Spirit who can remove the veil of unbelief allowing us to see with 20/20 spiritual vision. We need to open the Word of God and humbly ask the Holy Spirit to bring instruction, insight, and understanding for life. Let's not be found guilty of implying that it is "God's chart" (His Word) that is flawed!

It is amazing how we can read familiar Scriptures for years, and then suddenly a passage comes alive to our spirit with great meaning. We see what we have never seen or heard before, and understanding ignites a new depth of love for Jesus, the living Word. How often He sharpens our senses or corrects a blurred image in a moment of divine inspiration! It could be an "a-ha" moment as the dots of the Bible seem to connect to broaden our understanding or reveal a divine truth. One spiritual principle seems to explain another and suddenly we "see"! Deeper and more profound understanding may also come when we receive a timely word of scriptural encouragement. The Holy Spirit, given the invitation and the opportunity, will sharpen our spiritual eyesight and hearing to grasp the awesome dimensions of the kingdom of God. Is that what we are seeking?

Deafness is Hard to Admit

The ability to hear the Lord is a huge dilemma for all in the body of Christ. It is probably true to say the majority don't expect to hear the Lord speaking to them personally. This, however, makes no sense when we have a speaking God who calls each of us to incline our ears to hear Him! The Holy Spirit communicates wonderful spiritual insight to those who walk closely with Him, and it is an inspiring experience to hear a clear word from God about a situation or circumstance. But, be careful to never separate God's voice from His Word.

A Visit to the Audiologist

I married later than most at the age of forty-nine, and God's lovely gift to me was a gorgeous elderly gentleman named Des. We had been lifetime friends and found each other when he was widowed in August 2006. What a precious, loving, tender and gracious man. God demonstrated His love in His choice!

After a few initial visits, it was evident that, whilst Des looked switched on to all I had to share, not all I had to say was registering. It was as if a filter covered his ears. Some may call that wise, selective hearing! It was fine when we were close to each other, but when we were at a short distance or an object separated us some of what was communicated went by the wayside. However, he was totally unaware how his deafness affected me or others. Normally, it would not have mattered much, but Des was now entering a new world of ministry, and the ability to hear well was vitally important.

I was unsure how to handle this sensitive issue – the last thing I wanted was to upset or hurt him. So I made it a matter of prayer and waited God's time. There was a period of several months when he would turn the TV volume up, and I would turn it down. I often found myself repeating instructions or saying, "Did you hear what I said?" Sometimes he would even answer questions I had not asked! I played that one to my advantage for a while—that was fun. But more than all he would complain that people didn't speak clearly, that they mumbled.

However, Des soon realised he was missing a lot of what was going on and agreed to a hearing test. Of course, I wasn't slow in grabbing the opportunity to make the appointment. Our visit to the audiologist revealed the uncomfortable truth about the extent of his hearing loss. Surely, even Des could not argue with the audio levels portrayed on the computer? Yet, amazingly, he maintained that his hearing wasn't the problem as much as that people didn't speak up!

Finally, he was persuaded that he needed hearing aids. When they were fitted, the audiologist tested the levels of the new digital hearing devices to make sure they were functioning well. As he twisted some knobs to make adjustments Des leapt from his seat protesting, "Hey, it's far too loud!" It was the quickest I had seen him move all day! The patient audiologist smiled knowingly and calmly said, "Mr Whitmore, I have just set the level to what is considered normal hearing". Out of sight, I was grinning from ear to ear. There was a pause, followed by a deep sigh of resignation as Des swung his chair swiftly to face me. I quickly adjusted my gleeful expression. Gathering himself with that familiar sharp intake of air to steady his voice, a sheepish grin crept across his tense face. "Have I really been missing so much?" he asked with great resignation. There was no man so sweet; his humility ignited love, and I just melted! It took a long while for his brain to adjust to hearing the normal levels of noise again, but it was marvellous to see how he persevered.

When we married, Des moved from Kent in the southeast of England into my home on the south coast in West Sussex. He never made a fuss about the upheaval and change, but he did make it known he missed the birds in his Kent garden! He was absolutely convinced there were no birds in my garden because of the local cats. No amount of concrete evidence supporting the presence of birds would make him believe otherwise. Of course, he could not hear them! Astonishingly, after he started using his hearing aids, he tried to persuade me the birds had suddenly returned! What could I say?

For sure, when you are deaf, you do not know what you are missing; if you knew what you were missing, you would not be deaf! It is easy to become offended and defensive when our hearing is questioned. Many a domestic argument revolves around what was said and heard. It is hard to accept that we hear less than perfectly, and it is easy to blame everything and everyone else.

Can you imagine how God feels when, metaphorically speaking, we tell Him there are no birds in His garden because our impaired hearing cannot detect them? Jesus, in this parable, wants us to not only recognise that we are spiritually deaf, but more importantly, understand *what causes it,* and allow Him to do something about it.

According to Jesus, it is sin, the "rocks" and "thorns" in our hearts, which cause spiritual *blindness* and dullness of *hearing.* Equally it is sin, "rocks" and "thorns" that dull all our *spiritual senses.* We lose our *taste* for things of the kingdom and stand aloof from His *touch,* and we *smell* less than sweet! What and how you hear, and indeed what you miss, will determine spiritual growth.

Respond to What You Hear

Jesus knew that this parable of the kingdom of God had the power to bring dynamic change, but sadly in the superficial majority it changed nothing. There was no spiritual discernment of what He was talking about; they did not have a clue. Later, Jesus explained to the twelve and those close to Him (Mark 4:10) that He knew His words meant nothing to the crowd, because there was no evidence of repentance. In other words, hearing on its own meant nothing – it was empty and futile. Churches are full of hearers! However, God expects hearing that leads to transformation of mind and heart. The absence of sincere change sadly exposes an ignorance of true repentance.

In *Holiness, Truth, and the Presence of God* (1986), Francis Frangipane writes about repentance: "Some measure of repentance always precedes the coming forth of the living Christ in a person's life. To "prepare" and "make ready" is the purpose of repentance. Let us be sure we understand: John the Baptist's repentance did not merely make men sorry, it made men ready (John 1: 6). True repentance is to turn over the soil of the heart for a new planting of righteousness or directives from God. It is a vital aspect in the overall sphere of spiritual maturity. To truly change your mind takes time and effort. John's command to the Jews was to "bear fruit in keeping with your repentance" (Matthew 3: 8). Let us also realize that repentance is not over until fruit is brought forth. In effect, John was saying, "Cease not your turning away from pride until you delight in lowliness. Continue repenting of selfishness until love is natural to you. Do not stop mourning your impurities until you are pure". He demanded men keep on repenting until fruit was manifested. And if you will be holy, you will continue in repentance until you are holy."

On the Outside or on the Inside? A Mystery or a Message?

Are we an "outsider" or are we an "insider" to truth? By now, the crowd – those to whom Jesus referred as being "on the outside" – was gone. Jesus was alone with the twelve, together with a few others, helping them understand what the majority missed in the parable of the sower. There is such a lovely principle here. Jesus gives special explanation and insight to those who intentionally draw close to Him to learn. To the serious, teachable, committed disciple, the Holy Spirit will open treasures that casual, occasional, lazy, and lethargic believers will simply miss.

> Mark 4: 11a: "And He said to them, 'To you it has been given to know the mystery of the kingdom of God; but *to those who are outside,* all things come in parables …'" (NKJV).

We are really without excuse; we have heard so much yet understood so little. There has never been a time when so much teaching has been so readily available in churches, in books, on DVDs, CDs, TV, and the Internet. Most of us have sat under inspired teaching, seeing and hearing in spade loads, yet sadly, in comparison to what we have heard and seen, our lives have remained independent, immature, unchanged and disobedient, spiritually lacking in the apprehension and comprehension of truth. This is evidenced by low levels of spiritual maturity, empty prayer closets, deficiency in godly character, pettiness, stinginess, double-mindedness, and a casual indifference to the authority and power of the Word of God.

How can we hear so much yet remain unchanged? In the parable of the sower, Jesus leaves no doubt as to what the problem is, where it lies, and what hinders deep spiritual awareness, reception, and passion. It is to our advantage that Jesus does tell us; we need to know. Surely we want to know what is holding us back and stunting growth?

In 2012, the United Kingdom had the wettest summer on record. Floods ruined homes all over the country. From the comfort of my living room I watched the rain come down in torrents. The lawn disappeared under the flood of water, and a large pool formed. It could not drain; the ground had been saturated by weeks of rain. Plants rotted due to the overdose of what should have been nourishment. There was much more goodness available than the soil could ever productively digest. Is this a picture of our spiritual lives?

There is no doubt that Jesus longs for every believer to see with *Holy Spirit perception* and to hear with *Holy Spirit understanding*. He longs to dispense truth to our hearts, and to see the kind of spiritual growth that He suggests in the parable, thirtyfold, sixtyfold, and a hundredfold. But according to Jesus, that sort of growth will only occur in the life of one whose life is surrendered, whose mind is open to be taught and whose heart is clean.

The glaring difference between those who superficially see and hear to those who see and hear with perception and understanding is simply this—obedience and transformation of heart. Are we being transformed or are we the same as we have always been? We need courage to face this head on. Let's be prepared for a spiritual awakening in this study. Jesus said in Mark 4: 13: "Do you not understand this parable? How then will you understand all the parables?" (NKJV) Hidden within this parable are important principles of the kingdom waiting to be revealed. Jesus desires that the "mystery" of the kingdom of God becomes a personal, life-changing "message".

A Selah Moment

Let's pause to think and consider.

Prayer

"Lord Jesus, I kneel before You because you are my Lord and I am Your servant. You are my teacher; I am the learner. I long for a spiritual awakening. Awaken my senses to truth and help me grow in understanding. Unveil the eyes of my heart and help me see; unstop my ears to hear Your voice. Thank you that You not only plan that I grow spiritually, but that You create that growth within me by the Holy Spirit. Yes, Lord, I want to grow. Amen".

Questions to Consider and Answer

Think about your five senses: sight, smell, hearing, touch, and taste.

- If you were to give a score out of ten, one being poor and ten being excellent, how would you score each of your natural senses? Take one at a time and note your response in your notebook.
    - Now write down the five senses on a separate piece of paper and give it to a close and trusted friend. Ask him or her to mark out of ten how he or she perceives your natural senses.
- Compare answers and explore discrepancies or differences. Make notes.
- Repeat the same process for your spiritual senses.
    - How well do you *see* truth?
    - How well does your sense of *smell* recognise good and evil?
    - How well do you *hear* the Lord?
    - How responsive are you to God's *touch*?
    - How discerning are your spiritual *taste* buds?

- Now write down the five *spiritual* senses on a separate piece of paper and give it to a close and trusted friend. Ask him or her to score your spiritual senses.

Life Group

Within your group:

1. Explain why you scored your *natural levels* of sensitivity in sight, smell, hearing, touch, and taste as you did.

    a. How did your trusted friend score you? How did you feel when you asked him or her to make this assessment? What were the differences? Do you agree with your friend's assessment? Be honest about how you feel.

2. Explain why you scored your *spiritual levels* of sensitivity in sight, smell, hearing, touch, and taste as you did.

    a. How did your trusted friend score you? Do you agree with his or her assessment? Were you encouraged and/or challenged?

3. How would you like your life group to pray for you? Be specific.

    a. Listen carefully to each one's request. Remember confidentiality.

    b. Pray.

    c. Close with a time of thanksgiving to the Lord.

4. Before you finish, pass round *the packet of seed* your nominated person brought to the group. Each one should take one seed, take it home, and plant it. At the end of the discipleship study, each one should bring the new plant, or a photo of the plant, to the group.

Scripture for Meditation

"Therefore lay aside all filthiness and overflow of wickedness, and receive with meekness the implanted word, which is able to save your souls. But be doers of the word and not hearers only, deceiving yourselves" (James 1: 21–22 NKJV).

Chapter Two:

Growth According to Pattern

Read Mark 4: 1–29

Don't be tempted to skip this, let the whole passage soak into your spirit once again. We are going to consider the following passage:

> "And He said, 'The kingdom of God is as if a man should scatter seed on the ground, and should sleep by night and rise by day, and the seed should sprout and grow, he himself does not know how. For the earth yields crops by itself; first the blade, then the head, after that the full grain in the head. But when the grain ripens, immediately he puts in the sickle, because the harvest has come'" (Mark 4: 26–29 NKJV).

We have already seen that grasping kingdom truth to the point of transformation of heart requires more than hearing a message; it requires perception, understanding and application. Growth happens when truth penetrates to a deeper level of mind and heart, a depth which is only accessible to the Holy Spirit. Let's be clear, every disciple of Jesus should be growing.

The apostle Paul says: "These things we also speak, not in words which man's wisdom teaches but which the Holy Spirit teaches, comparing spiritual things with spiritual. But the natural man does not receive the things of the Spirit of God, for they are foolishness to him; nor can he know them, because they are spiritually discerned" (1 Corinthians 2: 13–14 NKJV). So, let's pray as we enter this chapter: "Lord, teach me about spiritual growth".

God's Pattern for Growth

Our passage of Scripture reveals something so simple yet so profound. God has ordained a preset order and plan for growth; it is a reproductive pattern that never varies. First of all, seed must be sown, and then it germinates, and later the plant pushes through the soil toward the light, growing to its full potential. A blade is formed, and then the head, and then the full grain in the head, and only then is it harvested. God set this pattern in motion at creation. According to His covenant, He will uphold the pattern of sowing and harvesting until the end of time. Read Genesis 8: 22.

In the beginning when God created all living things, He gave them the ability to yield seed that would grow and multiply their species. All seed would reproduce according to its kind. Think about it, God only had to create one pair of elephants!

> "Then God said, 'Let the earth bring forth grass, the herb that yields seed, and the fruit tree that yields fruit according to its kind, whose seed is in itself, on the earth'; and it was so. And the earth brought forth grass, the herb that *yields seed according to its kind,* and the tree that yields fruit, whose seed is in itself according to its kind. And God saw that it was good" (Genesis 1: 11–13, NKJV, emphasis added).

What is supernaturally created within every seed causes it to know exactly what to do; it doesn't need an instruction manual. "Of course", you say, "that isn't rocket science!" It is obvious what happens to seed; we've seen fields of wheat. Yes, it is obvious to the natural mind; even the crowds around Jesus saw that much! However, Jesus was communicating a much deeper message, which was lost on the majority. God's seed, His living Word, performs *just like natural seed when planted in the soil of our hearts.*

It knows exactly what it is and what it should become. It is preset with the power to effect new birth, bring deliverance, and cause healing in body, soul, and spirit, and it is "preset" to produce righteousness, fruitfulness, and multiplication. If this is true, why do the majority of the people in Jesus' parable miss out? Why are so many of us missing out? This should provoke some serious thought.

There are a number of things to emphasise from Mark 4: 26–29 that will help us lay a firm foundation for greater understanding.

1. **God planned that His seed be planted *in us*.**

Please take note that the destination of His seed is "in us". He is eager to sow and bed His seed-Word into the lives of His disciples; He seeks hearts that are ready to receive His Word.

- Do we expect the arrival of God's seed?
- Do we think about *how* it will enter us?
- Is the "soil" of our heart receptive?

Planting implies the seed is put into the depth of ready soil; it penetrates the soil and puts down roots.

2. **God's DNA is in His seed.**

God's seed has within it *the eternal attributes of the character of God.* Just as an apple seed will produce an apple tree, so God's righteous seed, planted into good soil, will produce His righteous character and nature in us. When it is planted in our hearts it prompts us to do right because righteousness is in its very nature.

The Holy Spirit embeds God's Word so that it is engrafted (James 1: 21). Engrafted means to insert; to join on; to fix deeply. Jeremiah 31: 33 says that in the New Covenant the Holy Spirit will put the law of God (Torah—Hebrew: God's teaching, instruction and guidance) in our minds and write it on our hearts. In other words, God plans for His eternal Word to literally become part of us! We will examine this further in Chapter 4.

It is the Spirit and the Word that empowers and directs us not only to do right, but to have *the desire to do right*; to act justly and walk humbly with our God. When we have God's seed living within us, we no longer need the external law (on tablets of stone) to show us what righteousness is; we have God's Word within us giving clear teaching, instruction and guidance to our mind and heart. Thus, we are not dependent on our own ability and strength to please God; it is God's righteous seed taking up residence in our hearts that produces righteous attitudes and behaviour.

This has serious implications regarding the tolerance of sin within the body of Christ. God's seed does not tolerate sin; it hates sin. We must consider what it means if we have no hatred of sin.

The apostle Paul says in Galatians 5: 18–21 that the works of the flesh (sin) are evident:

- Breaking covenant marriage vows and going off with someone to whom you have no right
- Having sex outside marriage
- Committing other sexual sins
- Having idols in your life
- Engaging in occult practices
- Letting your temper rage on those you meet, or those within your own household
- Seeking to have your own way
- Gossiping and causing division and strife
- Never being satisfied with what you have
- Getting drunk or promoting drinking parties

We are reminded that, "Those who are Christ's have crucified the flesh with its passions and desires. If we live in the Spirit, let us also walk in line with the Spirit" (Galatians 5: 24–25 NKJV).

3. **God planned that His seed would be fruitful in our heart.**

From the moment God's seed is planted in our heart there follows a powerful supernatural cycle of steady and orderly growth, predestined to fruitfulness. God doesn't simply throw seed randomly into the air for those who can be bothered to catch it. He sows by hand with love and precision, piercing the soil of a seeking heart. He isn't casual. The combination of the ways to bed His seed into a receptive heart, such as teaching, biblical meditation, preaching, testimony, study, reading and fellowship, is intentional and targeted. Every seed is precious. Every seed is His voice. We may hear teaching, and then later, we hear someone else give a testimony about exactly the same passage of Scripture or thought. It is as though God is reinforcing the lesson He wants us to hear and learn. It reminds us of 1 Corinthians 3: 6–7: "I planted, Apollos watered, but God gave the increase. So then neither he who plants is anything, nor he who waters, but God who gives the increase" (NKJV).

The farmer does not stay up at night wondering what the seed will produce or how fast it will grow. That would be a waste of time! He knows he cannot influence its pattern of growth or what it becomes. The farmer goes to bed knowing the seed he has planted will become exactly what it is destined to be. Can you imagine a farmer sowing wheat and worrying that pumpkins will grow instead? No, he has confidence in the seed; there will be no surprises. We can have exactly the same confidence in the growth-cycle of the Word of God. God's seed is living and active, so prepare for an explosion of the kingdom of God in your heart!

4. **Growth is always visible.**

According to Mark 4: 21–22, the word was not sown to be "hidden under a bed". Nothing is hidden in farming; the golden stalks swaying gently in the wind tell us everything about what the farmer planted in the field. Seed will yield fruit, it is seen and the harvest will be enjoyed by all who eat it.

As true as this is for the farmer, it is true for every single disciple of Jesus Christ. Growth is always seen. However, nothing in means nothing out! The field of our heart will be barren, and our laziness will also be seen and cause others to go hungry. The Bible calls this slothfulness. This is *not* the plan of God for His seed! Every disciple of Jesus is responsible to feed and nurture himself. But a disciple is also responsible to grow God's seed in his/her heart to supply, feed, and build up others.

If we never give opportunity for God to sow His seed into our heart, we cannot be a fruitful vibrant Christian – there can be no pretence, it is obvious, there are no golden stalks of wheat swaying in the wind! We may kid ourselves, but God is not fooled. A large percentage of believers do not even open their Bibles at home; God's "seed" sits in the "packet" on the shelf! This parable surely convicts us. We must give prime time to God and allow Him to sow His Word into our lives through regular reading, study, meditation, fellowship, and prayer.

It is incredibly sad to see empty and barren fields in believers' lives. Have you ever wondered why there are so many spiritually impoverished believers? The answer lies in the parable of the sower.

2 Corinthians 9: 8–11 says, "And God is able to make all grace abound towards you, that you, always having all sufficiency in all things, may have abundance for every good work. As it is written: 'He has dispersed abroad, He has given to the poor; His righteousness endures forever'. Now may He who supplies seed to the sower, and bread for food, supply and multiply the seed you have sown and increase the fruits of your righteousness, while you are enriched in everything for all liberality, which causes thanksgiving through us to God" (NKJV).

5. **God planned for many seeds.**

Like the farmer, when God sows He sows for future harvests. The farmer always thinks about the following harvests; He has multiplication in mind, and so does God. The biblical principle behind the production of "many seeds" is that God commands truth to be passed from one generation to another; we receive to pass it on.

You may have been struggling with feelings of low self-esteem having been hurt by fellow Christians. God, who is moved by your suffering, sends out a word of encouragement through one of His available servants. His intention is that you hear it, and that it falls into the soil of your heart. That seed of encouragement from God's Word pierces through the darkness and despair; like a shaft of healing light, it penetrates your emotions. You feel the warmth of God's embrace; you may even weep as the Holy Spirit pours God's love and acceptance into your heart. During the following months you notice other things happening that shape and rebuild your confidence and trust in God. A positive change has happened in your heart, and you feel more assured.

Soon, someone else who feels small and insignificant "coincidently" crosses your path. With heightened sensitivity, you notice the heaviness in their body language, and you are amazed to find the Holy Spirit leading you to share the very same Scripture that helped you so powerfully.

2 Timothy 2: 2 puts it this way: "And the things that you have heard from me among many witnesses, commit these to faithful men who will be able to teach others also" (NKJV).

Don't you see? Not only has God's seed born fruit in you for your benefit, God's seed is being multiplied for the building up of someone else. The whole process starts when you lay down your life before the Lord for Him to heal and restore, and then you lay down your life to bless someone else. Whatever God's seed provides for you, be it encouragement, correction, comfort, healing, cleansing, forgiveness, provision or protection, God plans that it reproduces through multiplication, thirtyfold, sixtyfold, or a hundredfold, for the benefit of others, and for the glory of His name. Too readily we just seek "a word" for ourselves.

In John 12: 24–25, Jesus said, "I tell you the truth, unless a grain of wheat falls to the ground and dies, it remains only a single seed. But if it dies, it produces many seeds. The man who loves his life will lose it, while the man who hates his life in this world will keep it for eternal life" (NKJV).

6. **The farmer understands seasons and understands time.**

He knows that what is planted today will not sprout tomorrow; there are appointed seasons for the growth of seed. So it is with the Word of God planted in us. Sometimes it takes years to produce fruit and develop spiritual maturity in particular areas of our lives. The process may involve the repetition of lessons in the school of discipleship until the power of God's seed finally breaks through. God designed fellowship with fellow believers for that purpose. We grow and develop as we rub shoulders and learn humility, patience and longsuffering. No one has ever acquired these virtues in isolation!

7. **The farmer does not know how the seed sprouts and grows. He just knows it does.**

Jesus says that "when the crop permits" (Mark 4: 29 NASB) the farmer immediately puts in the sickle, because the harvest has come. The kingdom is like this. We don't know when or how seed sprouts and grows, but we know that it does by what is seen.

"When the crop permits" is a striking phrase used in the New American Standard Bible. When God's Word has come to fullness, and it is time to harvest the fruit of what that Word has produced, it becomes evidently "full" and "ripe". There is always a "fullness of time", whether it is a fullness of time to share an insight God has given, a fullness of time to make a change, or a fullness of time which represents readiness for service. Church and mission leaders need great sensitivity to discern the fullness of time. They need to recognise who is ready for leadership, or to teach, preach, and share with others what has become life to them. In other words, it will be evident when one has ripened to maturity and readiness for service—God's fullness can be seen. Proverbs 18: 16 says, "A man's gift makes room for him and brings him before great men" (NKJV).

This also carries a caution! For the sake of fast-tracking a new believer, or a young person, or filling a gap in ministry, don't harvest too early. Many have been released into responsible leadership positions and significant ministry without the fruit of godly character having been formed in them. It is fraught with danger, not only for the person concerned but for those they lead. Leading others in matters he or she has little understanding of, or experience in, can have devastating consequences. Many inexperienced and immature leaders, struggling with pride and independence, use control to secure submission and obedience. Many get hurt. We need courage, patience and love to wait for "when the crop permits".

A Selah Moment

Let's pause right here. We have quite a lot to think about.

Prayer

"Lord, I give You praise and heartfelt thanks for determining and planning for spiritual growth in my life. I want to be Your true and committed disciple. Teach me more about how the seed of Your Word can come to maturity in my heart. Help me be disciplined and diligent in study, worship, prayer, and meditation upon Your Word. Multiply Your seed in me so I might grow maturely to feed and nurture others. Amen".

Questions to Consider and Answer

- What spiritual growth are you seeing in your life? Journal your thoughts.
- Are you growing, and how do you know you are growing?
- What is your favourite passage of Scripture, and how have you seen God bring it alive in your spirit?
- How has that Scripture been reproduced through you in the life of someone else?

Life Group

Begin your life group today with the following Scripture: "As the rain and the snow come down from heaven, and do not return to it without watering the earth and making it bud and flourish, so that it yields seed for the sower and bread for the eater, so is my word that goes out from my mouth; it will not return to me void or empty, but will accomplish what I desire and achieve the purpose for which I sent it" (Isaiah 55: 10 NKJV).

- Discuss this verse (no more than twenty minutes).
    - To what is the Word from His mouth likened?
    - Why does God send a Word from His mouth?
    - What are the benefits of being a recipient of a Word from His mouth?

- During the past year, when and how did you hear a Word from God's mouth?
- Close with prayers of thanksgiving for what you have heard.

Scripture for Meditation

"And He Himself gave some to be apostles, some prophets, some evangelists, and some pastors and teachers, for the equipping of the saints for the work of ministry, for the edifying of the body of Christ, till we all come to the unity of the faith and of the knowledge of the Son of God, to a perfect man, to the measure of the stature of the fullness of Christ; that we should no longer be children, tossed to and fro and carried about with every wind of doctrine, by the trickery of men, in the cunning craftiness of deceitful plotting, but, speaking the truth in love, *may grow up in all things into Him* who is the head – Christ – from whom the whole body, joined and knit together by what every joint supplies, according to the effective working by which every part does its share, causes growth of the body for the edifying of itself in love" (Ephesians 4: 11–16, NKJV, emphasis added).

CHAPTER 3:

God's Seed Gives Us A New Identity

Read Mark 4: 1–29 and

In this chapter we cast our net further afield into the Word of God. There are many related Scriptures that help us understand the parable of the sower, and none more so than the passage from the Apostle John's epistle. Read this carefully and keep in mind the following questions:

- Who or what is it that gives us our identity?
- "Who are you?"

Read 1 John 2: 29–3: 9

> "If you know that He is righteous, you know that everyone who practices righteousness is born of Him. Behold what manner of love the Father has bestowed on us, that we should be called children of God! Therefore the world does not know us, because it did not know Him. Beloved, now we are children of God; and it has not yet been revealed what we shall be, but we know that when He is revealed, we shall be like Him, for we shall see Him as He is. And everyone who has this hope in Him purifies himself, just as He is pure."

> "Whoever commits sin also commits lawlessness, and sin is lawlessness. And you know that He was manifested to take away our sins, and in Him there is no sin. Whoever abides in Him does not sin. Whoever sins has neither seen Him nor known Him. Little children, let no one deceive you. He who practices righteousness is righteous, just as He is righteous. He who sins is of the Devil, for the Devil has sinned from the beginning. For this purpose the Son of God was manifested, that He might destroy the works of the Devil. Whoever has been born of God does not sin, *for His seed remains in him;* and he cannot sin, because he has been born of God" (1 John 2: 29–3: 9, NKJV, emphasis added).

Who Are You?

I was *born naturally* of my dad's seed. My dad, James (Jim) Rowland, is with Jesus. Most who knew him would say, "Gosh, you are just like your father!" I enjoy whatever it is they are seeing because I'm proud to be like him. But when they say such things, what are they referring to? I've asked that question, and the consistent answer is, "You talk like him, you walk like him, your humour is so like his, and you have the same talents in training, communication, music, and art. Yes, Jan, you are like him". Statements like that should not be surprising because I have the DNA of my father's seed. There is no doubting whose child I am.

When I was *born-again,* I was supernaturally born of God's seed. I received the DNA of my heavenly Father's seed, Jesus Christ. This gave me a brand-new identity; God's implanted seed made me a child of God. Being born-again had a dramatic effect on my character and behaviour. Just like Jim Rowland's DNA was seen in me as I grew up, so my heavenly Father's seed creates characteristics that are "just like Him". I don't have to pretend to be like Him, or by my own effort try to copy His characteristics. They are being supernaturally formed and developed in my spirit, by the Holy Spirit, as I grow in grace and in the knowledge of Him. I am delighted to be growing up to be like my heavenly Father! I am a child of God, and I am so proud, and somewhat relieved, when people tell me, "You are just like your heavenly Father".

We Have a New Identity

God's seed planted into our hearts is Jesus, and Jesus is the Word of God. The moment we repent and receive the holy Seed we are born into a new family, the family of God. We are reconciled to God and now we are the "children of God". The Holy Spirit makes our dead spirit alive to its new identity in Christ Jesus! This parable teaches us that while God's seed is in the womb of our hearts, "we don't know what we shall be, but what we do know is that in the fullness of time it will be revealed, and *we will be like Him*" (1 John 3: 2, NKJV, emphasis added).

When the farmer sows seed in a field he expects a harvest in full keeping with what he has sown. So it is with God. He sows His seed into our hearts, and true to farming principles, the seed grows and produces according to its divine DNA. It is the DNA of "God's seed" that gives the newly born person in the kingdom of God his or her brand-new family identity. This is such good news for people who come from dysfunctional earthly families!

So what will a person who is born of God become and look like? This is a powerful question. Let's take the answer directly from our passage.

- "We shall be like Him" (1 John 3: 2 NKJV).
- "If you know that He is righteous, you know that everyone who practices righteousness is born of Him" (1 John 2: 29 NKJV).
- "Whoever has been born of God does not sin, for His seed remains in him; and he cannot sin, because he has been born of God" (1 John 3: 9 NKJV).

It is easy to identify people who are born of God:

- They are unmistakably God's child.
- They practice righteousness. It can be seen in their godly thoughts, words, and deeds. They talk, think, see, feel, behave, and walk just like Him.
- Sinning is no longer the person's orientation: "He cannot, because he is born of God".

It is God's seed that develops the character of Jesus in us, calling and directing us to live righteously, and giving the power and ability to do so. But, there is something more: God's seed also creates a longing to purify our hearts. The word "pure" here is *hagios* (Greek) and comes from the same root as "holy". It describes a person or thing as clean, modest, pure, undefiled, morally faultless, and without blemish. The resident heavenly "seed" compels inner purification and produces pure behaviour and pure attitudes. "And everyone who has this hope in Him purifies himself, *just as* He is pure" (1 John 3: 3, NKJV, emphasis added).

No Pretence is Necessary

There are many people in our churches on a Sunday who believe it is their duty to be good; it is expected of a Christian. Therefore, outward appearance and behaviour is important to them. They reign themselves in to moderate and control their outward behaviour to do and say the right thing. They make sure they are 'Christian' and are seen to perform their 'church duty' in a Christian manner. It is external Christianity—people behave as if "being good and acting right" is wholly dependent on their own effort and self-control. They carry with them a sense of self-righteousness. It is easy to spot, because during the week you see them acting very differently from when you saw them in church! Actually, this is legalism, a form of religion, about which Jesus brought correction to the Pharisees. It places the onus on self-ability to be good and do good, and makes hard work of living a Christian life. Thankfully, the kingdom of God holds much better news than self-effort! When God's seed is within us it declares us righteous, and, *it, by the Holy Spirit's power,* produces God's righteousness, love, and purity.

Paul put it this way in Galatians 2: 20 "It is no longer I who live, but Christ lives in me; and the life which I now live in the flesh I live by faith in the Son of God, who loved me and gave Himself for me" (NKJV).

When we are born again, we are born of God's seed; God places His manifest and holy presence within us. Our lives are enmeshed as *one with Him*; I in Him and He in me. From the moment of planting, every single ounce of spiritual power condensed in that small seed is destined to change me into the likeness of Jesus. That is why a person who is truly born again finds it impossible to habitually carry on sinning. A spiritual battle ensues that only finds resolution and peace in true repentance and surrender. God's seed is pure and brings light; it challenges and exposes every area of darkness that is so destructive. Every born-again believer will experience the purity of God's seed crying out for release from the filth and defilement of sin. Conviction of sin becomes a relief as it leads to repentance. Repentance washes away sin and sets our heart free. This is not about trying to beat ourselves into some sort of holy submission; it is wholly about God's seed giving us the deep desire, power, and ability to live "just like He does".

> "No one who is born of God will continue to sin, because God's seed remains in him; he cannot go on sinning, because he has been born of God" (1 John 3: 9 NIV).

This Scripture is not saying that once we are born again we are perfect. We are still capable of being tempted into *sinful attitudes and behaviour* because of the weakness of our flesh and the strength of Satan's temptation. However, when we are born-again we do not live from our flesh; we choose to live from our spirit which is enlivened by the Holy Spirit. We have God's resident power which keeps us from sinning *habitually* (where sin has had controlling power over us). Put another way, God's presence makes it impossible to *habitually* live in sin without feeling guilt, which ultimately leads us to repentance. The pulsating and holy seed of God releases new authority and power to crucify our flesh; we are no longer characterised by "lawlessness" (1 John 3: 4). To be lawless is to be without God's law.

When we give the Holy Spirit opportunity to plant and embed the Word in our hearts, spiritual authority ("exousia") is established. It is like adding tough inner muscle, courage and strength to our weak frame—we have God's might. Additionally, purifying power ("dunamis") is released in our lives. As we are daily filled with the Holy Spirit, dunamis power enables us to live in the Spirit, walk in the Spirit, and be led by the Holy Spirit. As God's seed blossoms in our hearts, it governs, shapes and transforms our *outward* behaviour and conduct. This is the *normal Christian life* for all believers.

We Are Called to Be Distinct

Are we full of integrity and purity? It is sad when believers habitually use foul language, habitually tell dirty jokes, habitually view pornographic images, habitually flirt with the opposite sex or habitually persist in an immoral lifestyle. They offer a weak apology, as if that makes it better, but at the same time they display the hardness of heart that says, 'I still have this right'. The same could be said of excessive drinking and partying; believers take license, using the excuse of meeting with people who have no Christian commitment. Meeting with people is good, but becoming drunk and coarse to identify with them is sinful. If we are walking in the Spirit we will know this is wrong. The seed of God is pure and brings forth purity.

God Sows With Joyful Expectation

Mark 4: 14 tells us the seed is the Word of God. We can picture God, as a farmer, going out with a pouch full of Word-seed. He is full of joy and expectation as He fills His hand and broadcasts intentionally into the soil of our heart. He knows its powerful, good and nourishing properties can lead to the joy of an unrestricted and healing union with Him. He knows His seed has the power over sin and death. He also knows His seed will bring healing and restoration, binding the broken-hearted and releasing the captive. It is a life-changing force.

Are you truly born-again? Scripture could not be clearer; you either have Father's DNA because you are born-again of His seed, or you don't. If you are born-again of God's seed, you will be growing in His likeness, joyfully, freely, and willingly practicing righteousness; sinning will be hard because the authority and power of God's seed will not permit that which He knows will separate you from Him.

A Selah Moment

Let's pause. We have some serious questions to think about and answer.

Prayer

"Lord Jesus, am I truly born-again? Am I like You? Am I practicing righteousness and holiness? Am I flirting with sin? Are there any areas of my life where I am trapped in habitual sin? I want to reckon with this passage of Scripture and be assured that I am truly born-again of Your seed. I want, Lord, to live my life from the dynamic life, authority, and power of Your seed within me. Help me, Lord. 'Create in me a clean heart, O God, and renew a steadfast spirit within me. Do not cast me from Your presence, or take Your Holy Spirit from me. Restore to me the joy of your salvation and grant me a willing spirit, to sustain me. (Psalm 51: 10–12, NIV). Amen".

Questions to Consider and Answer

- Are you truly born-again of God's seed? When was the day you chose to enter into covenant with Jesus, the day you gave your life over to Him?
- If your answer is no, and you sincerely want to know the authority and power of God's seed transforming and directing your life, pray this special prayer:
    - "Lord, this chapter has undone me and uncovered what lies at the root of my life; I have never truly been born-again. I've been frustrated and I've made an absolute mess trying to be a good Christian by my own effort and strength. Forgive me, Lord. I want to turn from independence to giving my life to You. Amen".
- Let the Holy Spirit lead you in *thorough* repentance. Ask the Lord what it is in your life that offends Him. Listen to the Holy Spirit as he lays His finger on sin in your heart.
- Pause here to ask forgiveness for specific sins – name them one by one. When you know you have fully confessed, pray:
    - "Lord Jesus, plant Your eternal seed in my heart; I forsake all others and all things in giving my life wholly to You".

- Pause here to name the people and things you are forsaking – name them one by one. This is not only a declaration to God, it is a declaration to Satan himself. When you are ready, give thanks:
    - "Thank you, Lord, I receive Your seed! You are my Father. Send the Holy Spirit to fill and empower me. Cause me to grow to be like You. Amen".
- If you answered yes, that you are truly born-again, answer the following:
    - How do people know you are a child of God? What has changed in you? What of God is seen in you?

Life Group

- How do people know you are a child of God? Can others see God's righteousness in how you live your life?
- What area of temptation do you struggle with? How does it affect your life? Be specific.
- Describe how it feels when the Word of God washes you clean. You may want to share when that happened to you personally.
- Close in prayer: encourage one another to pray freely and honestly. By now there will be a deeper level of trust, which allows this kind of freedom without risk of judgment.

Scripture for Meditation

"Who can understand his errors? Cleanse me from secret faults. Keep back Your servant also from presumptuous sins; let them not have dominion over me. Then I shall be blameless, and I shall be innocent of great transgression. Let the words of my mouth and the meditation of my heart be acceptable in Your sight, O LORD, my strength and my redeemer" (Psalm 19: 12–14 NKJV).

Chapter 4:

The Quality of the Seed

Read Mark 4: 1–29

Don't be tempted to skip this reading. By now the structure of the text should begin to embed in your heart.

Let's pray: "Lord, speak to my heart afresh through this wonderful passage of Scripture. Show me the things that, as yet, I haven't seen or understood. Thank you so much that You are the One leading me to discover vital keys to possessing the kingdom of God. Amen".

The Seed is the Word of the Kingdom

When Jesus began to explain the parable of the sower to His disciples He said, "The sower sows the word" (Mark 4: 14 NKJV). Matthew's rendering of the same parable says the seed is, "the word of the kingdom" (Matthew 13: 19 NKJV). Luke's rendering says the seed is, "the Word of God" (Luke 8: 11–12). The "Word" (of God), "word of the kingdom" (of God), and "the seed" (of God) are synonymous terms in this parable.

The kingdom of heaven came to earth in the person of Jesus Christ, and He declared the word of the kingdom. The destination of the kingdom of heaven *is our hearts*, where God establishes His rule, reign, and authority by His living Word—Jesus Christ.

John 1: 14 says, "And the Word became flesh and dwelt among us, and we beheld His glory, the glory as of the only begotten of the Father, full of grace and truth" (NKJV).

Luke 17: 21 says, "The kingdom of God does not come with observation; nor will they say, 'See here!' or 'See there!' For indeed, the kingdom of God is within you" (NKJV).

How Does the Bible Describe the Word?

Let's consider:

1. What are the properties and features of God's seed?
2. How does God's Word act like seed in our hearts?
3. What does God's Word accomplish in us?

Take time to look up every Scripture and as you study remember that this is *the very seed* God wants to plant in *your* heart. It will be helpful to make notes in your notebook to share with your life group.

- The Word of God *strengthens* – Psalm 119: 28
- The Word of God *revives* – Psalm 119: 25
- The Word of God is a *sword* – Ephesians 6: 17b
    - It cuts through and exposes the lies of the enemy.
- The Word of God is *counsel* – Isaiah 46: 9–10
    - It counsels us and we are able to give sound counsel.
- The Word of God *gives answers* – Psalm 119: 42
- The Word of God gives *understanding* – Psalm 119: 169
- The Word of God is *precious* – Psalm 119: 72; 1 Samuel 3: 1; Psalm 12: 6

    - It is like having a treasure trove within.
- The Word of God is *right* – Psalm 33: 4; Psalm 138: 2
    - When it is planted within our hearts by the Holy Spirit we have spiritual authority (exousia).
- The Word of God is *creative* – Psalm 33: 6
    - By the Word of God the world was made.
    - The Holy Spirit releases creative power (dunamis) in and through our lives.
- The Word of God *quickens* life – Psalm 119: 49–50
    - When we are down and in despair, it releases comfort and gives us hope.
- The Word of God is a *lamp* to our feet and a *light* to our path – Psalm 119: 105
    - We can hold the Word of God in our hand like a lamp, shining light on our present position; we can see where we are. It also lights every step forward so we know how to proceed, react, and plan.
- The Word of God gives *life in our afflictions* – Psalm 119: 107
- The Word of God gives *joy* – Psalm 119: 162
- The Word of God is *pure* – Psalm 119: 140
    - The Word purifies and cleanses our lives.
- The Word of God *sanctifies* – John 17: 17
    - It separates us unto Him. It consecrates our lives to His service.
- The Word of God *runs swiftly* and is able to *melt* the snow, frost, and hail – Psalm 147: 15–19

- The Word of God gives *direction* – Isaiah 30: 21
    - We will hear a word behind us, saying, "This is the way, walk in it".
- The Word of God *changes the impossible to the possible* – Luke 1: 37
- Hearing the Word of God *creates faith* – Romans 10: 17
    - The Holy Spirit uses the Word of God to awaken a response of faith within us, and it is the reliability of the Word of God on which we rest our faith for salvation. The words of Scripture are the words of eternal life (James 1: 18; 1 Peter 1: 23).
- The Word of God *changes us within* – 1 Thessalonians 2: 13
    - It has the power to redeem and change our lives.
- The Word of God is *living, active and sharp* – Hebrews 4: 12
    - It penetrates and discerns the thoughts and intents of a person's heart. It separates soul and spirit.
- Constant study of the Word of God *trains us in discerning good and evil* – Hebrews 5: 14
    - We can know the difference and make the right choices.
- The Word of God *stands forever* – Isaiah 40: 8
    - When everything else withers and fades, God's Word endures.
- The Word of God is *sin resistant* – 1 John 3: 9
    - When planted within, its presence and power stops us from sinning.
- The Word of God is *incorruptible* – 1 Peter 1: 23
    - We have been born again of incorruptible seed.

That list is incredible. That is life-giving seed and *that seed* is the 'word of the kingdom'—it powerfully creates kingdom life within. When God plants His seed in our hearts, we need never wonder what's next, what to believe, what to do, what is good and what is evil, or how to respond to the many choices and decisions of life. The wisdom of God will already be growing within us. The Holy Spirit uses God's Word to teach and lead us because the Word of God is *everything* God says it is.

Pastor Jack Hayford, Church of the Way, California, says, "We owe our new birth to the power of God's word and the Holy Spirit's activation of its power. The [parable of the sower] tells us the 'seed' that has produced new life in us is the Word of God, which has begotten us again by the Holy Spirit's power [Titus 3: 5] and made us members of God's new creation [2 Corinthians 5: 17]. The power of God's Word, the Holy Scriptures, has the power to bring spiritual life to all who open themselves to its truth".

Jesus said, "When He, the Spirit of truth, has come, He will guide you into all truth; for He will not speak on His own authority, but whatever He hears He will speak; and He will tell you things to come" (John 16: 13 NKJV).

The Blessing of Torah—the Word of God

When we were born-again we entered into the "new covenant" with God, through Jesus' shed blood (Matthew 26: 28). Jeremiah 31: 31–34 explains what the new covenant is:

> "Behold, the days are coming, says the LORD, when I will make a new covenant with the house of Israel and with the house of Judah — not according to the covenant that I made with their fathers in the day that I took them by the hand to lead them out of the land of Egypt, My covenant which they broke, though I was a husband to them, says the LORD. *But this is the covenant* that I will make with the house of Israel after those days, says the LORD: *I will put My law in their minds, and write it on their hearts; and I will be their God, and they shall be My people.* No more shall every man teach his neighbour, and every man his brother, saying, 'Know the LORD,' for they all shall know Me, from the

least of them to the greatest of them, says the LORD. For I will forgive their iniquity, and their sin I will remember no more" (NKJV, emphasis added).

The LORD contrasts two covenants. In the first, *God's law* was written on tablets of stone (the covenant given to Moses on Mt. Sinai) and in the second, *God's law* is written within—"in our minds and on our hearts" (the new covenant in Jesus blood). The contrast is striking—the first was *external,* the second *internal*—both, however, are written by the same hand, God, the Holy Spirit.

But, what is *"God's law"*? We may immediately think of the Ten Commandments and be partially right. We may also recoil at the word "law" thinking only of restrictions, the "law of the land", or a list of do's and don'ts. However, the true meaning holds much better promise than that! *"God's law"* is translated from the Hebrew word "Torah", meaning *teaching, instruction and guidance.* In the new covenant God promises to write His divine teaching, instruction and guidance in our hearts by the Holy Spirit. What a wonderful promise!

In its fullness Torah is a detailed description of who God is and how God works. It describes His nature, character and ways. It reveals how He defines holiness. It presents His expectations for His people. It is a reflection of His perfect will and wisdom. It is a group of teachings that our gracious heavenly Father has given to instruct us in our community life, as well as in our personal walk as believers. It teaches us how to live in relation to one another. Psalm 1 uses exactly the same word—Torah—and it reminds us that when we find delight in God's law (Torah), meditating upon it day and night, we will ever be strong and fruitful! It is our "how to live" manual. It represents the fullness of what God would have us learn of Him. *This* is the dynamic seed God sows into the soil of our hearts!

King David expressed what he felt about God's teaching, instruction and guidance:

"Oh, how I love Your law—*Torah—teaching, instruction and guidance*! It is my meditation all the day. You, through Your commandments, make me wiser than my enemies; for they are ever with me. I have more understanding than all my teachers, for Your testimonies are my meditation. I understand more than the ancients, because I keep Your precepts. I have restrained my feet from every evil way, that I may keep Your word. I have not departed from Your judgments, for You Yourself have taught me. How sweet are Your words to my taste, sweeter than honey to my mouth!" (Psalm 119: 97–103, NKJV, emphasis added).

Boaz Michael, the President and Founder of First Fruits of Zion writes: "In the narrowest sense, the first five books (Genesis, Exodus, Leviticus, Numbers and Deuteronomy) are called the Torah, the "teaching" of Moses. But in a broader sense, all of Scripture is Torah, because all of Scripture is the "teaching" of God. Please note that this isn't a new idea. In rabbinic usage, the word Torah also includes the rest of the Scriptures (keeping in mind that for the rabbis, this meant the Old Testament alone). The Psalms and the Prophets, and even the little scrolls of Esther, Jonah, and Ruth are all Torah. They are all teaching—all part of God's Torah. That's why Paul can say, "It is written in the Torah," and then quotes from the Psalms. The Master himself does the same. For Christians, the Torah is even broader than it is for the rabbis—the Gospels are Torah. Paul's writings are also Torah. The epistles are Torah. The Revelation of John is also Torah. It is all teaching which builds upon, and agrees with, the first chunk of God's Torah as delivered through Moses."

Let's cherish and delight in the whole Bible, OT and NT—the whole integrated and bountiful counsel of God. God's Word is a lamp to our feet and a light to our path (Psalm 119: 105).

We are not saved *by keeping God's eternal law*—that is legalism. We are saved by putting our faith in Christ Jesus and the finished work of His blood upon the cross. However, it is true to say that *we keep God's law because we are saved*. We are compelled to do so by the authority and power of God's law which is now within us! We are also compelled by our love for God to keep it! The more we know how much God has forgiven us, the more we love Him. The more we love Him, the more we want to obey and please Him. Love for God ignites when we undeservedly experience His great mercy, love and forgiveness. We are distinguished as God's people by the abiding power, ability and activity of His Word renewing our thinking and transforming our hearts (Romans 2: 29). It marks us out as His people!

Our heavenly *Father* sent the *Seed* of God, which is *Jesus,* and we are transformed into His likeness by the *seed* of God, which is the Word of God, which is the word of the kingdom. This is why Romans 12: 1–2 says:

> "I beseech you therefore, brethren, by the mercies of God, that you present your bodies a living sacrifice, holy, acceptable to God, which is your reasonable service. And do not be conformed to this world, *but be transformed by the renewing of your mind,* that you may prove what is that good and acceptable and perfect will of God" (NKJV, emphasis added).

Let's not be law-*less (Torah-less),* living without the teaching, instruction and guidance of God's Word. If we do, the Bible warns that we will become lukewarm and perish. We must teach God's people to love the truth, be responsible, and to endure to the end.

> Matthew 24: 9–14 "Then they will deliver you up to tribulation and kill you, and you will be hated by all nations for My name's sake. And then many will be offended, will betray one another, and will hate one another. Then many false prophets will rise up and deceive many. *And because lawlessness will abound, the love of many will grow cold.* But he who endures to the end shall be saved" (NKJV, emphasis added).

> 2 Thessalonians 2: 7–10 "For the *mystery of lawlessness* is already at work; only He who now restrains will do so until He is taken out of the way. And then *the lawless one* will be revealed, whom the Lord will consume with the breath of His mouth and destroy with the brightness of His coming. The coming of *the lawless one* is according to the working of Satan, with all power, signs, and lying wonders, and with all unrighteous deception among those who perish, *because they did not receive the love of the truth,* that they might be saved" (NKJV, emphasis added).

Even Jesus kept God's commandments because He loved His Father! He lived by His teaching, instruction and guidance.

Matthew 4: 4 says, "It is written, 'Man shall not live by bread alone, but by every word that proceeds from the mouth of God'" (NKJV).

John 15: 10 says, “If you keep My commandments, you will abide in My love, just as I have kept My Father’s commandments and abide in His love” (NKJV).

John 14: 15–16 says, “If you love Me, keep My commandments” (NKJV).

The outcome of God’s teaching, instruction and guidance being put *in our minds* and written *on our hearts* by the *Holy Spirit* is transformation and knowledge of Him. We are changed to be like Him. Hallelujah!

A True Story: Appointment in Jerusalem

Claudia Merkle, a single German missionary, was placed in a small group whilst participating in a “Listening Prayer Seminar” in Europe. The small group had gathered to practice and apply listening skills in “Hearing the voice of the Lord”. True to the way of the Lord, He spoke to those who were listening, and Claudia, who was totally uncomfortable with the process, heard members of the group describe three specific pictures, ideas, and impressions they insisted were for her. One spoke of “sirens going off”, another mentioned the words “the Holocaust” and a third person spoke of “the power of the Holy Spirit being within us”. For her, the combination of the three made no sense, and she found aspects of what was shared somewhat insensitive to her German background. She shelved all three.

In April 2009, needing time off from her mission work, Claudia heard that Mission Encouragement Trust (MET) was hosting a retreat for single workers at Notre Dame de Sion in Ein Kerem, Jerusalem, Israel. She was one of thirty missionaries accepted for the retreat.

In praying for the retreat, I, together with Mintie Nel (Directors of MET), received a “seed word” from the Lord that the theme of this particular retreat should be, “Dwelling in Covenant”. It certainly was special to be teaching about “covenant” in the very land given by God in covenant to His people, Israel! Additionally, you cannot imagine how excited we were when we learned Notre Dame de Sion, a Catholic retreat centre, was founded by a Messianic Jew whose central message was “walking in covenant” with God!

A Visitation from God

It was a beautiful, crisp, bright morning as all the missionaries gathered for worship and Bible teaching. There was an intense sense of God's holy presence; the atmosphere was pregnant with His power. Without warning, the quietness was shattered by the sound of a piercing siren, increasing in tone and volume. I was forced to stop teaching while the room fell silent. One of the Jerusalem workers called out, "It's okay; it is Holocaust Memorial Day today. The siren is just reminding us!" It was so appropriate to pause in honour of and respect for God's chosen people who paid the highest price for bearing the mark of covenant on their lives. God Himself stood observantly in our midst, and one could hardly breathe. The siren stopped, we prayed, and we carried on with our teaching session on "the new covenant". Sitting quietly in the crowd, Claudia's eyes filled with tears. Unbeknown to us, the Holy Spirit was reminding her of what He had said in the "Listening Prayer Seminar" so long ago.

It had been a dramatic morning, so we sent the other missionaries outside to reflect on what the Lord had been saying. Claudia found a quiet spot in the garden overlooking the Judean hills. In the stillness her Bible fell open to Acts 1: 4: 'Don't leave Jerusalem until you have received the promise of the Father'. The text leapt from the page and excitement filled her heart! She did not want to leave Jerusalem without the gift that God had in store for her, but, she wasn't sure how it would happen or what it would be.

While the missionaries were enjoying their personal time with the Lord, our staff team gathered to pray for them. We sensed we were in an extraordinary moment, and we needed to hear direction from the Lord. How should we sensitively proceed with the rest of the morning? As we waited the Holy Spirit clearly instructed us to meet together again, as a group, and pray for anyone who would like to be filled with the Holy Spirit. We still had no idea what was happening with Claudia.

We gathered the whole group and opened the floor for people to share what God had been saying to them. Hesitantly, Claudia came forward; she was excited, thoughtful, and scared, all at the same time. Her eyes brimmed with tears as she unfolded the story about her journey from the Listening Prayer Seminar to the retreat. Two people, moved by her testimony, spontaneously reached out to pray for her, and as they did the Holy Spirit came powerfully upon her, filling her to overflowing with joy.

Later in the retreat she shared of Jesus changing her heart – removing the old heart of stone and giving her a new heart of flesh. She said, "When I received the Holy Spirit, the darkened room of my heart was flooded with light. I have been living in the Old Covenant, believing Jesus had died and rose again, but not letting Him change my heart, still trying to keep His commandments in my own strength. It was hard work, and I have been struggling".

When you realise the lengths God went to bring transformation to Claudia's life, you can only bow humbly before the Lord and say, "Me too, Lord". She was transformed by God's seed bearing fruit within her. What an awesome God.

The evening of that extraordinary day, we welcomed Pastor Reuven Ross into our retreat to share some insights and understanding about what God was doing in Israel at that time. We had a boisterous time of worship with many celebrating newfound liberty in Jesus; there was great freedom in expressing adoration of Him. Out of the corner of our eye we could see Claudia dancing! We know she hated dancing, so it was quite something to see this lovely German girl set free. She told us God had made her so happy that she simply had to jump around.

When Reuven spoke, he told us what happened in the "prayer tower" of the King of Kings Assembly that morning. 'This morning, a group of workers from my fellowship met for a time of prayer on the fourteenth floor of a very high building in Jerusalem. As we started, God told us to take time to pray specifically for the Mission Encouragement Trust (MET) retreat in Ein Kerem. Then He gave us a Bible verse, Acts 1: 4: "And being assembled together with them, He commanded them not to depart from Jerusalem, but to wait for the Promise of the Father, which, He said, you have heard from me". We prayed that God would pour out His Spirit on you this morning.'

The atmosphere was electric as astonished faces registered that Reuven and his prayer group would not have known what their prayers had accomplished in our retreat that morning. God had orchestrated an awesome sequence of events.

God Sows His Seed and Guides it to Fullness

This is a remarkable story that has four testimonies in one. Let's take a moment to reflect on it in the light of God's seed being sown into hearts.

Firstly, many months before the retreat, God told us that the theme would be, "Dwelling in Covenant". It was God's seed-word. When we arrived at the retreat centre we were told by the Catholic nuns that it was a Messianic Jew who had purchased the land and established the buildings. He was convinced that that particular piece of land had been given by God in covenant. It was remarkable that we were led by the Holy Spirit to teach about God's covenant love on covenant soil! It was so reassuring to be in the right place at the right time by God's appointment.

Secondly, there was the "seed-word" (the picture and impressions) that God had spoken to Claudia. She may have been a reluctant recipient but God sowed His seed, even into a hesitant heart. It was when Claudia came to the retreat that "what God had said" sprouted and matured to fullness, pressing through the surface of her objections, preconceived ideas and unbelief. She had heard "*the sirens* going off", the explanation of what the sirens were for—*Holocaust* Memorial Day—and she was powerfully *"filled with the Holy Spirit"*. It had all begun many months previously in the Listening Prayer Seminar in Europe. God sowed His word into her heart, and in the fullness of time He fulfilled every promise in dramatic fashion, right down to the tiniest detail.

Thirdly, there was the moment during the retreat when we did not know how to handle what God was doing. Our MET staff joined us in waiting upon the Lord on behalf of the missionaries. In that divine moment of prayer, God sowed another seed-word into our hearts through Acts 1: 4: "Pray for those who would like to be filled with the Holy Spirit". That seed-word quickly came to fruition. Many of the missionaries requested the 'laying on of hands' and were gloriously filled with the Holy Spirit. Several experienced miraculous healings—backs were healed and legs grew!

Fourthly, there was the testimony of Reuven Ross. Whilst waiting on the Lord in Jerusalem, God spoke a seed-word via Acts 1: 4: "Pray that those enjoying the MET retreat will not leave Jerusalem until they have received power". Exactly at the same time as his prayer group was praying in the prayer tower in central Jerusalem, just three miles away in Ein Kerem God was indeed pouring out His Spirit, and answering their prayer!

It was a dramatic and life-changing day! Surely these events, just like the events in the Acts of the Apostles, encourage us to prioritise significant time with the Lord, to be filled with the Holy Spirit and devote ourselves to His Word? If we give opportunity and allow the Holy Spirit to put God's seed into the soil of our heart by means of disciplined waiting, listening, fellowship, reading, study, meditation, and memorisation, all the amazing attributes and characteristics of the Word will start to manifest within. We will be cleansed, purified, pruned and transformed, bearing much fruit. We also may be instrumental in sowing God's seed into the life of another. Plant the Word and you are guaranteed to be spiritually alive, with a "ready word in and out of season" (2 Timothy 4: 2) cultivated in our heart. Will you allow it to produce "what it is" within your heart?

A Selah Moment

Let's pause and think about all this.

Questions to Consider and Answer

- Return to the list under the heading, "How does the Bible describe the Word?" About which of the statements can you say, "Yes, I've seen that in my own life"? Tick those with which you can identify.
- Prepare a testimony about receiving a specific word from the Lord and how He fulfilled it.
    - When and how did you hear from the Lord?
    - Record how you acted on the revelation, and how it worked out.

Prayer

"Lord, it is amazing what ability and power You have put into the nature of Your seed. My prayer is that I will be transformed by the teaching, instruction and guidance of Torah—Your eternal Word. I deeply desire that the authority and power of Your Word will be effective in my life. Amen."

Life Group

- Enjoy listening to each group member's testimony.
- At the end of each testimony take a few minutes to identify which description of God's seed you recognised in the testimony. List the aspects shared.
- When all have shared, review your list and enjoy a time of praise and thanksgiving for all that God is doing in your lives.

Scripture for Meditation

> "The entrance of Your words gives light; it gives understanding to the simple" (Psalm 119: 130 NKJV).

Part II: The Soil

INTRODUCTION:

It is Time for Ground Clearance

We are now a good way into this study. In chapters 1–4 we laid a solid foundation for chapters 5–12. Congratulations on your perseverance in study and faithfulness in fellowship with your life group. Let's remind ourselves that the focus of this study is spiritual growth. We want to grow in our knowledge of God, His character, and His ways and experience spiritual transformation in our lives. There is no doubt the Father, Son, and Holy Spirit are giving their full attention, willing and helping us on.

Remember, there is no shortcut or fast track to growth; spiritual growth follows God's created pattern in the natural cycle of seed. So far we have recognised from Jesus' teaching that:

1. God's seed needs to be planted to obtain a harvest.
2. God's seed needs good soil and the right depth to produce. The reception of God's seed will always mean death to our flesh life.
3. Growth is methodical, systematic, and evident; first the seed goes in, and then roots take hold. When the roots are set, the seed releases a surge of strength, pushing its stalk up through the soil towards the light and the warmth of the sun. One seed becomes many seeds in the head, producing a harvest. Nothing is hidden.

4. The rewards of growth reach far beyond the field of our own heart. What God produces in us can feed and sustain others.

In chapters 1–4 we studied the nature of God's seed. Now we will study the quality and condition of the soil. How can the soil be prepared and its quality be improved? Every gardener knows the value of preparing the soil, of weeding and pruning to galvanise a new burst of life. It is no different in the garden of our heart. In the parable of the sower, Jesus teaches us there are things in the heart that actively resist, clutter, hinder and impede the fruitfulness of His seed. Our heavenly Father gives loving attention to what needs to be removed and pruned because He knows the quality and quantity of the harvest depends on that essential process.

In John 15, Jesus describes His relationship with the disciples in these very terms: "I am the vine, and my Father is the vinedresser. Every branch in me that does not bear fruit He takes away; and every branch that bears fruit He prunes, that it may bear more fruit".

For many years, I observed with secret envy and a mocking spirit those who were experiencing spiritual richness; they didn't just have Bible knowledge, they possessed that vibrant life elusive to me. It was obvious that their growth was not plucked out of the air or visited randomly upon them. This was no half-baked commitment; they devoted themselves to God's Word and prayer, zealous to let the Lord shape and change their heart. When they shared insights from the Bible it was full of life, it wasn't a dry theory. They increased financial giving to sacrificial levels and looked to give away possessions to help others. It was never too much to give up a Saturday to serve someone else. To be holy was something they prized and were never ashamed of. To be distinct from the world was an honour. They were clearly experiencing a depth of relationship with God I knew little about, but I was magnetically drawn to them; I wanted what they had.

In those days, I learned the most valuable lesson of my life, and it was this: observation of and desire for spiritual growth were not enough. If I wanted what they possessed, I would have to engage with the Word and "put *my own* hand to the plough". I was spiritually lazy, so to receive such spiritual blessing by some sort of magical transference would have been just the ticket! But it wasn't going to happen that way. God had a discipleship training school tailor-made for me, and it started with counting the cost. Discipleship costs everything. Is it worth it? When you experience the joy of thirtyfold, sixtyfold, and a hundredfold return, you never ask that question again!

The radical change began with some targeted "ground clearance". My daily life, as it was, had no extra time or space; I was a full-time professional woman. So I started by giving up something that possessively consumed prime resources, time, and attention: my hobby of music. Music was my life and joy. Nothing rivalled practising piano and cornet/trumpet for two hours each day, as well as participating in concerts and music groups. I had one goal: to get to the Royal Academy of Music in London. It was an honourable pursuit, but it filled my mind and possessed my heart, and it was a hindrance to the dedicated time required to foster spiritual growth. My life had to be reprioritised to God's order.

I was twenty-six years old. Nobly, and not without some considerable pride, I determined the time I had devoted to practising the piano and the cornet I would spend in prayer and Bible study. I thought that would impress God! My instruments were put up for sale, and they sold in just three days. I secretly hoped it would take a while or that perhaps God was only looking for my willingness to give them up – you know, like Abraham and Isaac! But there was no mistaking His resolve, and to cut even deeper into the flesh of my heart, the Holy Spirit instructed me to give all the money to missions. Until that point I had thought putting a pound coin in the offering was being generous!

Before this, my prayer life had consisted of five minutes in the car on the way to work and sometime during the day I quickly read the *Every Day with Jesus* devotional by Selwyn Hughes. I was a flabby believer, doing very little spiritual exercise. I expected others to feed me. It had never occurred to me that I should learn to feed myself spiritually. In the beginning, entering into a new spiritual exercise routine was sheer hard work—there wasn't much joy around!

How faithfully God walked that road with me; He was my personal trainer. Five minutes of prayer on the run soon became fifteen on my knees, and fifteen soon increased to an hour flat on my face. And that time was matched in study of the Word. I thought it was going to be an endless drag, but the more I pursued communication with God and His Word, the more God pursued me. And the more I experienced a new lease of life in prayer, the more I experienced the power of the Holy Spirit transforming my life. I felt alive and purposeful. God developed a beautiful intimacy with His child, and I experienced His overwhelming love, affirmation, and approval. Music quickly faded into the background. I think it was significant that five years after making some radical lifestyle changes, I was not only able to hear the call of God to full-time ministry in missions, but I was able to know the joy of obedience.

Today, all over the world, there is a dynamic move of the Holy Spirit which is causing believers to radically reassess the cost of discipleship. Weary of the world, spiritual mediocrity and church programmes, believers are found in small groups, often in homes, crying out to the Lord for change. They seek the company of those who walk closely with the Lord in truth, without compromise. Insatiable hunger and thirst for righteousness has drawn them back to in-depth study of the Word and utter dependence on the Spirit. Rather than "having a message" they desire to *be the message*. Spiritual fervency is once again spreading like wild-fire!

Paul describes it like this: "You are our epistle written in our hearts, known and read by all men; clearly you are an epistle of Christ, ministered by us, written not with ink but by the Spirit of the living God, not on tablets of stone but on tablets of flesh, that is, of the heart. And we have such trust through Christ towards God. Not that we are sufficient of ourselves to think of anything as being from ourselves, but our sufficiency is from God, who also made us sufficient as ministers of the new covenant, not of the letter but of the Spirit; for the letter kills, but the Spirit gives life" (2 Corinthians 3: 2–6 NKJV).

How do you sign up for this kind of invigorating growth? Start by counting the cost of discipleship, then make personal sacrifice, and then pick up your cross and follow Jesus. Give away, break the shackles of the world, turn away from sin and devote yourself wholeheartedly to the Word of God and prayer. Zeal for the Lord means relinquishing those things that resist and hinder the very growth you passionately desire.

Let's remind ourselves again how Jesus put it in Mark 8: 34–37: "When He had called the people to Himself, with His disciples also, He said to them, 'Whoever desires to come after me, let him deny himself, and take up his cross, and follow me. For whoever desires to save his life will lose it, but whoever loses his life for my sake and the gospel's will save it. For what will it profit a man if he gains the whole world, and loses his own soul?'"(NKJV)

Evolving in the Presence of Fire

In a serious pursuit of God we will experience the Refiner's fire! In October 1999, David Herring wrote an article for NASA, "Evolving in the Presence of Fire", as part of the Boreal Ecosystem Series (http://earthobservatory.nasa.gov/Features/BOREASFire). He said, '[The year] 1998 was an extreme [one] for wildfire activity throughout the North American and Russian boreal forests. More than 11 million hectares [110,000 square km] burned that year. Although most people regard fire as a destructive force that should be fought and quickly extinguished, the fact is the boreal forest evolved in the presence of fire and adapted to it. Fire is the mechanism by which the forest is continually regenerated. Fires consume dead, decaying vegetation accumulating on the forest floor, thereby clearing the way for new growth. Some species, such as the jack pine, even rely on fire to spread their seeds. The jack pine produces 'seratonous' (resin-filled) cones that are very durable. The cones remain dormant until a fire occurs and melts the resin. Then the cones pop open and the seeds fall or blow out".

Nobody wants to experience a fire; fiery ordeals are devastating. A match is lit or a spark flies, and in a matter of minutes life as we knew it is destroyed. Adultery, loss, chronic illness, death, bankruptcy, betrayal, redundancy, a personal attack, tragedy, theft, all have the capability of starting a fire of huge proportions in our lives. The deep sense of violation and loss shatters and debilitates. The fiery nightmare changes the landscape of our lives forever. However, after a time and almost inconceivably, new life pushes up through the soil in the midst of the dead and burnt vegetation. Fresh and green shoots appear in the sacrificed soil. It is a miracle—God brings new life from the ashes! (Isaiah 61: 3a) Fire does what nothing else can do, it strips us of self. God, who is not distant or unaware, waits patiently and compassionately to swoop to our aid as He hears our cry of helplessness, resignation, and finally, surrender. Disciples of Jesus readily "evolve", they "unfold and open out", and they " develop" through the divine refining process. They become pure, meek, tender, gracious and merciful just like their Lord. For them the fiery ordeal is painful but it offers the promise of fresh and vibrant spiritual growth.

The sincere pursuit of God will take a path through fiery ordeals. Accept it. All the "greats" of the Bible would confirm that view. Greatness is produced through fire and greatness is always marked by a humility born of fire. In the following chapters we will discover that that sort of ground clearance is the price of fruitfulness. "My brethren, count it all joy when you fall into various trials, knowing that the testing of your faith produces patience. But let patience have its perfect work, that you may be perfect and complete, lacking nothing" (James 1: 2–4 NKJV).

Over the years the Holy Spirit has graciously shed penetrating light on my sinful actions, wrong and misguided thoughts and motives. He has lit a match on selfishness, harboured anger, pride, unforgiveness, sexual contamination, rejection, and idolatry. Sadly, at times I have responded to tests and trials with only retaliation, anger and resentment. In doing so I have made the refining process far more painful, slow and extended than it needed to have been. But, I have never regretted the pursuit of righteousness, holiness and redemption. It has forged a spiritual boldness in my heart. Spiritual reward far outweighs the pain of momentary hardship and affliction.

The purging of our heart is painful but it is all part of true discipleship. We can ignore and excuse many "skeletons in our wardrobe", but to do so accepts spiritual mediocrity as God's plan for our life. God doesn't "do" mediocrity. His plan is fruitfulness by our union with Him. So let's get going from chapters 5—11 and embrace some significant and worthwhile cleansing that breathes new and fresh life through our stuffy and stifled hearts!

Chapter 5:

A Hearing Heart

God's Word can only be as productive as the condition of our heart allows.

We begin this chapter by revisiting some provocative questions. If the seed that God is sowing is all the Bible declares it to be, why do we find ourselves often unaffected, indifferent, and unchanged? Where does the problem lie? We surely have to draw the conclusion that if there is nothing faulty or inadequate about God's seed, the problem lies with the soil in which the seed has been sown, our heart. Not too many believers want to look at the condition of their hearts and face heart issues, but according to the parable of the sower, spiritual growth is wholly dependent on their doing exactly that.

> "The heart is deceitful above all things, and desperately wicked; who can know it? I, the LORD, search the heart; I test the mind, even to give every man according to his ways, according to the fruit of his doings" (Jeremiah 17: 9–10 NKJV).

Saved and Satisfied

I clearly remember the day I gave my life to Jesus. I was seven years old attending the Salvation Army Sunday School in Gillingham, Kent,

United Kingdom. It was the day known as 'Decision Sunday' on the Salvation Army calendar. David Bean, our Young People's sergeant major, gave a simple presentation of salvation, and my young heart was strangely stirred by the message. Feeling as if the entire world was watching me, I nervously left my seat and walked fearful, shaking and alone to the front of the junior hall, and I knelt at the "mercy seat" (in the layout of every Salvation Army church this represents the mercy seat of the Ark of the Covenant; a holy place to meet with God). Emotion welled up from deep within. I simply believed what was said and asked Jesus into my heart; I felt clean and new.

I tucked my hand in Dad's as we briskly walked home that afternoon. My feet skipped, almost not touching the ground. My heart was full of joy. Excitedly, I told him about my new commitment, and although his introverted response was total silence, I realised my dad was choking back a swelling tide of thankful emotion. He firmly squeezed my hand, holding it so tightly that when he finally let go it was white. I was so happy my dad was proud of his daughter's decision; I liked to please him. I didn't realise it then, but I learned later that all heaven was on its feet that afternoon, rejoicing and praising the Lamb of God because a child called "Janice" had come to Jesus in Gillingham in the United Kingdom! I guess my dad felt that joy too.

In a sense I'd arrived, yet in reality the spiritual journey had only just begun. At seven, I didn't know much about life. I didn't need to – I was a child guided and protected by my parents. But in years to come, the natural journey of growing up was destined to attract its own trouble and storms. The innocence of childhood was lost as my heart battled the contamination of sin and the world, a battle in which I was often defeated with shattering consequences.

For many years I wrestled as close friends grew spiritually with leaps and bounds. I started well when I was first filled with the Holy Spirit, but in my twenties I lagged far behind, too paralysed to even acknowledge I needed to face the dark shadows in my own heart. For me the solution was evident—friends would just have to accept me the way I was, and in return I would tolerate their newly found "over the top" spirituality. I sarcastically hid behind phrases such as, "They are too heavenly minded to be of any earthly use", or 'One day they will wake up and come down to the real world". I was saved, and that was good enough for me. Of course I was wounded and hurt, imprisoned by Satan behind the walls of my heart. It is amazing how I excused such arrogance and pride!

Salvation had happened in a moment of decision, but transformation was going to take a while longer. I was to discover much later that whilst God, my Father, received me as I was, it was not His plan for me to remain as I was—wilful, deceived, and sinful. He had come to set this prisoner free! I was not only to be saved, I was called to be sanctified, and the process of sanctification brought me face to face with the deceitfulness in my heart. I realise now that if we have never considered our heart deceitful, we really are deceived and hardened!

Isaiah 53: 4; 61: 1 says Jesus shed His blood to bear my grief and carry my sorrows, to heal my broken heart, and to open the prison door and set my heart free.

If, in this season of discipleship, we determine to apply Jesus' farming principles to spiritual growth, we must be prepared to accept not only the blessing of God's seed, but also, the powerful and loving exposure of God's seed. There may well be some challenging "soil" problems to look at and acknowledge, but be absolutely assured that Jesus' heart is full of love for us. He will never expose our heart to betray, put us down, embarrass, or shame. He exposes the motivations, intentions, and deceptions of our heart only to bring us to freedom, healing, and full reconciliation with God our Father, with ourselves, and with others. Thankfully, He is the One who examines our hearts, and it is only He who knows how to turn over the soil with tender care and bring precision healing.

What is the Heart According to the Word of God?

Discipleship is all about the renewal of the mind and the transformation of the heart. But according to the Bible what is our heart? The Hebrew word "lev" (or "levav") appears 860 times in the OT. It means "heart", referring to the part of us that feels, hopes, grieves, loves, thinks, and decides. You could say that the heart is the combination of the soul (mind, will and emotions) and spirit. So, your heart is "you"– your personality.

Vine's Expository Dictionary of Biblical Words defines the heart as follows: "The 'heart' stands for the inner being of man, the man himself. As such, it is the fountain of all he does" (Proverbs 4: 23).

If we ask the Lord to examine the condition of the soil of our heart, we are, in fact, considering what it is in our soul and spirit that hinders, resists, or stunts our spiritual growth. What has contaminated our hearts? What keeps us from intimacy with Jesus?

Jeremiah 17: 9 says, "All his thoughts, desires, words, and actions flow from deep within him. Yet a man cannot understand his own heart" (NKJV). Deuteronomy 30: 6 says, "As a man goes on in his own way, his heart becomes harder and harder. But God will circumcise [cut away the uncleanness of] the heart of His people, so that they will love and obey Him with their whole being" (NKJV).

What is in Our Heart?

The parable of the sower makes us face the hardness, rocks, and thorns because Jesus loves us and longs to bring healing and reconciliation. What is the spiritual health of our mind, will, emotions and spirit?

We all have negative things that clutter our hearts, which, for one reason or another, we have never brought to the cross to apply the blood of Jesus. We are saved, but we still carry what Hebrews 12: 1 calls "*every weight and the sin which so easily entangles us*", which we should "*lay aside*". So few of us have ever been discipled in how to identify what entangles our hearts, let alone how to "lay it aside". Even after being a Christian for many years, we are still weighed down and "running the race that is set before us" (Hebrews 12: 1) with a limp! Spiritual growth is a long way behind where it should have been by now.

We all have reaction "buttons" that get pressed in adverse and stressful situations, causing varying degrees of internal and external "volcanic eruptions". Our reactive behaviour and attitudes betray what we carry on the inside. They reveal what we have chosen to "live with" rather than "lay aside", and everyone closely involved feels the negative impact of it. Satan loves to nurture his own seeds in our lives, and he will do anything to cause us to justify and maintain ungodly attitudes and behaviour, thus keeping us from the cleansing and healing power of the blood of Jesus. Make no mistake, Satan's plan is to kill, rob, and destroy believers (John 10: 10). God's plan of salvation is to root out and cleanse, redeem, and restore, bringing us to the fullness and completion of reconciliation with Himself.

A believer should not duck away from being renewed in the mind and transformed in our heart. To truly "believe" is to enter into a dynamic, growing, covenant relationship with the living God. We cannot spend the rest of our life just simply saying we are Christian and then go about life as we please. It is impossible to stand still, or stay on the sidelines as a spectator, while God's seed is present in a believer's heart. There is no neutral place; if we are not growing we are dying.

Read Mark 4: 1–29

This request comes with such repetition, but please read the whole passage once again. Ask the Holy Spirit to show and teach you deeper truth. The purpose of reading it over and over is to allow it to soak into your spirit.

Why Do Some Grow and Others Don't?

Jesus was constantly preaching the kingdom of God to large audiences, yet only a relatively small number, upon hearing His message, were moved from "seeing" and "hearing" to a deeper level of revelation. The majority who listened to His teaching only listened on a natural and superficial level, unmoved and untouched by what He shared. I wonder how many left Jesus that day saying, "That was a good message. He spoke well. I liked what He had to say. He definitely understands farming!" But their lives were unaffected; they carried on exactly as they had before.

That scenario is sadly played out in the lives of millions of believers all over the world every Sunday morning; they hear a fantastic message, beautifully and powerfully delivered, but it registers no change in attitude or behaviour. Life goes on exactly as it had before church that morning. It is a heart issue that God wants to address. Let's not kid ourselves; nothing is hidden from Jesus; He saw us go to church and watched us go home. This parable implies that He knows the exact state of our heart and whether or not the "fantastic message" brought us to humble repentance and transformation. One day we will be held accountable for what we did with what we heard. This should awaken the fear of the Lord! Meekness is a disposition of heart for all believers in Jesus Christ. We should have a soft and repentant heart to the end of our days.

Jim Bakker, the disgraced American TV evangelist who lost his television ministry after a series of sex and money scandals in the 1980's was reputedly asked, "What happened? Did you lose your love for Jesus?" Bakker reputedly replied, "No, I never lost my love, I lost the fear of the Lord."

Leading People to Repentance is Always Love

I have heard it said the word repent is "outmoded" in favour of a somewhat watered-down response like "sorry". However, the concept of biblical repentance is not easily modernised. The problem is you can be sorry about many things without any hint of change in your heart or behaviour. "I am sorry I hurt you" is so weak and superficial, when you might then see that person just move on to hurt someone else in exactly the same way. Repentance is marked by a deep remorse for sin, and it is accompanied by sincere contrition for the pain inflicted (Isaiah 55: 7; 57: 15). It is humility that recognises and confesses sin against God and others, taking ownership of wrong-doing by giving and receiving forgiveness. *Repentance births a noticeable change of heart* brought about by the Holy Spirit, and it is always followed by the "practicing of righteousness" (1 John 3: 29).

There is a high price to pay for neglecting God's persistent and faithful call to live repentant and holy lives. For both old and new believers, repentance is always God's path to spiritual growth and renewal. It is God's powerful cleansing agent that guarantees sweet union and intimacy with Him. Sadly, many believers do not realise that unrepentant, independent, and contaminated lives, even with hands raised in the air in worship or delivering prophetic words, are a sham, and God resists drawing near (Proverbs 15: 8a, 28: 9). "God resists the proud but gives grace to the humble" (James 4: 6 NKJV).

This farming parable is so direct in its message—the condition of our heart is exposed by what our life produces. The Holy Spirit of God brings forth fruit of righteousness; the spirit of the world brings forth the fruit of worldliness, sinful behaviour and attitude. With seed there is a short hidden season of growth beneath the surface, but eventually what is there will push through the surface towards the light and reveal itself. It will be seen for what it is, good or lacking.

It is within the same context that Jesus says, "Is a lamp brought to be put under a basket or under a bed? Is it not to be set on a lamp stand? For there is nothing hidden which will not be revealed, nor has anything been kept secret but that it should come to light" (Mark 4: 21–22 NKJV).

Just like farming, spiritual growth is measured *by what is produced,* not by empty words or good intentions. Growing in spiritual maturity in the kingdom of God is only measured by faithfulness and endurance to the end. Jesus did not want to condemn people; His tender heart of love appealed to them to understand the condition of their heart in order to bring them to healing, and new life in Him, through true repentance. *It is always loving to bring people to a recognition of sin and lead people to repentance*; to leave them in the bondage and darkness of sin is unloving, disrespectful, devaluing (of the person and the blood of Jesus) and potentially eternally destructive.

Four Soils – the Same Seed

Read Mark 4: 3–9 and Mark 4: 13–20

Underline or highlight every occurrence of the words 'fell' and 'hear'.

> "Listen! Behold, a sower went out to sow. And it happened, as he sowed, that some seed fell by the wayside; and the birds of the air came and devoured it. Some fell on stony ground, where it did not have much earth; and immediately it sprang up because it had no depth of earth. But when the sun was up it was scorched, and because it had no root it withered away. And some seed fell among thorns; and the thorns grew up and choked it, and it yielded no crop. But other seed fell on good ground and yielded a crop that

sprang up, increased, and produced: some thirtyfold, some sixty, and some a hundred" (Mark 4: 3–9 NKJV).

"And He said to them, 'Do you not understand this parable? How then will you understand all the parables? The sower sows the word. And these are the ones by the wayside where the word is sown. When they hear, Satan comes immediately and takes away the word that was sown in their hearts. These likewise are the ones sown on stony ground who, when they hear the word, immediately receive it with gladness; and they have no root in themselves, and so endure only for a time. Afterward, when tribulation or persecution arises for the word's sake, immediately they stumble. Now these are the ones sown among thorns; they are the ones who hear the word, and the cares of this world, the deceitfulness of riches, and the desires for other things entering in choke the word, and it becomes unfruitful. But these are the ones sown on good ground, those who hear the word, accept it, and bear fruit: some thirtyfold, some sixty and some a hundred.' And He said to them, 'He who has ears to hear, let him hear!'" (Mark 4: 13–20 NKJV).

In Mark 4: 3–9, Jesus highlights *four types of soil;* all four had seed *fall* upon them. There was no lack of seed "falling"; it fell on every type and it was all the same seed! This reveals the tender and impartial love of God, giving opportunity to everybody for life and spiritual growth. It should also be noted that *all* "heard" to some degree.

In Mark 4: 13–20, Jesus explains what the four soils represent, adding this interesting phrase: "*When they hear*". All four soils represent "hearing people", but only *one* out of the *four* groups was able to hear in a manner that brought fruitfulness. Jesus explains that there are various reasons why some people grow and others don't. He makes this diagnosis: hardness of heart, rocks, thorns, and unresolved issues compete with the growth of His living seed.

The parable records four different types of soil: the hardened wayside, rocky ground, ground with thorns, and good ground. Let's say it again, all four "heard" the same message about the kingdom of God; however, the message transformed the hearts of only a few. Everyone received the same seed with the same potential; it was only "the good soil" that bore fruit in keeping with the potential of God's seed.

In Mark 4: 15, the *hardened wayside* heard *superficially,* in one ear and out the other. In Mark 4: 16–17, the *rocky soil* heard *enthusiastically* but there was no depth of soil for the seed to root and when the sun came up the lack of a root system caused the plant to wither away. In Mark 4: 18–19, the *thorny soil* heard with *consideration,* but it had already been compromised by opponents and competitors. In Mark 4: 20 the *good soil* heard *productively* and what was heard bore fruit thirtyfold, sixtyfold, and a hundredfold.

It is possible to hear the Word of God without any revelation or penetration of heart whatsoever. According to Jesus the hearing of God's Word can only be as productive as the condition of our heart allows. So, friends, we simply have to let the Holy Spirit lead us in a time of careful and loving examination.

We Determine Our Own Measure

In Mark 4: 24–25, Jesus says, "Take heed what you hear. With the same measure you use [for hearing], it will be measured to you; and to you who hear more will be given. For whoever has, to him more will be given; but whoever does not have, even what he has will be taken away from him" (NKJV).

The context of these two verses is "hearing". The condition of our heart determines the measure of our spiritual perception and understanding! Jesus is saying *we set our measure of growth* because *we choose* whether to allow God to clean up our heart or not. God never overrules our choice. He longs that we choose His love, and His love longs to cleanse us of the devastating effects of the flesh, sin, and the world. When the heart is clean and consecrated, we are able to discern and see spiritual things of which we have never dreamt or seen before. The Lord has clear access to sow even more precious seed into our life. Purity of heart opens our eyes to see God (Matthew 5: 8). We grow from strength to strength. Why on earth do we want to hang on to the junk that contaminates our hearts when Jesus offers freedom and newness of life? Jesus says that to those who have the capacity to hear with understanding because they have chosen to cleanse their hearts, more understanding and revelation will be given.

This principle of "measured hearing" also works negatively. If we do not choose God's cleansing and continually fill our minds with the world's opinions and our own philosophies and ideas, we will have little sensitivity to the voice of God speaking His wisdom through His holy Word. Self-knowledge and self-aggrandisement replace the need to hear God's voice; we measure everything by ourselves, our superior knowledge or advanced education. We are self-opinionated. We don't need God to teach, instruct or guide us because we have already made up our mind! As a result, we lose whatever spiritual understanding we have.

These verses underscore that it is the condition of our heart that determines our ability to hear productively. What is in our heart is the key to growth, and this will be explored in the next few chapters. We need courage to deal with heart issues, but the eternal reward far outweighs the momentary discomfort and pain.

A Selah Moment

There is a lot to think about! I have such joy in my heart as I sense you are on the edge of finding the unique quality and power of God's eternal and precious life. I am reminded of what God said to Joshua recorded in Joshua 1: 7 and 11: "Only be strong and very courageous, that you may observe to do according to all the law which Moses my servant commanded you; do not turn from it to the right hand or to the left, that you may prosper wherever you go ... cross over this Jordan ..." (NKJV)

Prayer

"Lord, give me courage not to turn away or run from this critical moment in this discipleship experience. Help me face forward and give me strength to 'cross over this Jordan' into the promised land of blessing in Christ Jesus. How much have I been missing of what You have been saying over many years? Cleanse and change my heart; I want to leave behind my old life and fully embrace my new life in the kingdom of God.

"Lead me gently through the next stage of facing up to any hardness, rocks or thorns in my heart. I may have many unresolved issues from the past where I have not allowed You to examine many areas of my life. I long that my heart becomes good and fruitful soil. I need a thorough heart cleansing. Bring me to repentance. Change my heart, O God. Amen".

Questions to Consider and Answer

- At this juncture, what is God speaking to you about? Journal your answer in your notebook.
    - Be honest about what you are beginning to see in your own heart.
    - Give the Lord time to share what He sees in your heart.
- Which words would you use to describe your ability to hear spiritually?
    - Take some time to think this through and journal your responses.
- If "growth is the only evidence of life", describe how you have grown spiritually over the years.
    - What does spiritual growth really mean?
    - How do you measure that growth?
    - What progress have you seen?

Life Group

Using the answers to the questions you considered earlier, focus on two questions:

- What aspect has been most challenging in this study so far, and why?
- What evidence of growth does your life display?

Please leave thirty minutes at the end to pray for each other. Resist trying to sort each other out; the Holy Spirit is both willing and able to do that! To wrestle with truth is a great thing. You may well have far more unanswered questions at this moment than when you started, and that is fine. Learn to rest your unanswered questions in the hands of Jesus. In time you will come to greater enlightenment. Just support and affirm one another with unconditional love; your strength lies in walking this path together in openness and honesty.

Scripture for Meditation

> "Keep your heart with all diligence, for out of it spring the issues of life" (Proverbs 4: 23 NKJV).

CHAPTER 6:

Lord, Do I Have a Hardened Heart?

Read Mark 4: 4 and Mark 4: 15

> "And it happened as he sowed, that some seed fell by the wayside, and the birds of the air came and devoured it" (Mark 4: 4 NKJV).
>
> "And these are the ones by the wayside where the word is sown. When they hear, Satan comes immediately and takes away the word that was sown in their hearts" (Mark 4: 15 NKJV).
>
> "The devil comes and takes away the word out of their hearts, lest they should believe and be saved" (Luke 8: 12 NKJV).

As shocking as it sounds, there are people in whom God's seed has no effect. Jesus is not evaluating the power and ability of the seed; He is highlighting the tragic condition of a heart that provides no resting place for God's seed. In the hardened heart, there is no soft bed of receptive soil into which the Word of God can nestle and root; it is like a hard-packed dirt road, inhospitable and sometimes hostile.

Jesus tells us that those with hardened hearts hear the very same life-giving Word others hear, but where others are enthused and respond, it does not touch them. Their hearts remain unmoved and feel no compulsion to respond; they remain unchanged. This sort of hardness of heart, described by Jesus as a "pathway", provides an opportunity for Satan to "kill, rob, and destroy" any vestige of spiritual hope. It is tragic that Satan can so freely steal the very seed that has the potential to bring dynamic change to the life of the hearers.

It is tempting to conclude that perhaps God's seed-word, stolen by Satan, was simply not meant for those who did not respond; maybe it was just for the others. This is how we tend to judge 'messages' from the Lord: they both hit and fit, or we brush them off with, "It wasn't meant for me". How about asking deeper questions, such as, "*Why* did I get nothing from the message? Was it not for me, or *is there something in my heart* that resists the message?" These are questions a true disciple of Jesus would ask, but the hard of heart would probably rather judge the messenger than allow the message to examine them. There would be little or no inclination to admit the problem lies within them; typically they would deflect any personal responsibility by apportioning blame elsewhere. Hardened hearts seem to have well-organised built-in defence mechanisms that neither God nor fellow humans are able to penetrate. Tragically, this heart is closed.

So, the discipleship questions we must ask are:

- According to God's Word, what is hardness of heart?
- What causes it?
- How do we recognise this danger in our own lives?
- Is there any hope of it being changed?

Two Scenarios to Help us Understand

To help us examine what hardness of heart means, let's contrast two scenarios in the lives of the children of Israel. In the first scenario, hardness of heart was demonstrated in *unbelief,* which resulted in rebellion; in the second there was softness of heart demonstrated in *belief* or *faith,* which resulted in obedience and victory.

1. Israel in the Wilderness

Read Exodus 15, 16, and 17

The children of Israel lived in Egypt for 430 years. The favour they had once enjoyed steadily declined with every change of Pharaoh, deteriorating towards oppression and sorrow under the ruthless Egyptian taskmasters. The Bible tells us God saw, heard, and knew their sorrows (Exodus 3: 7). He appointed Moses to deliver them out of the hand of the Egyptians, to bring them up from that land of bondage into the Promised Land, a good and large land flowing with milk and honey. He sent Moses to set His people free. It was an awesome deliverance which is still celebrated in Israel today in obedience to the command of God in Exodus 12: 25. It is called the Lord's Passover (Exodus 12: 11–13). When the LORD (YHWH, Adonai) saw the blood of lambs on the doorposts of their homes, His wrath passed over them. The plague of death killed every firstborn child of the Egyptians, including those of Pharaoh's many wives, his household slaves, livestock etc., but could not enter to destroy the Israelite firstborn because they had applied the blood. What a beautiful picture of Christ our Redeemer, and what a lesson in terms of the power of *applying* the blood of the Lamb of God.

We Want to Go back to Egypt!

The exodus from Egypt was a solemn occasion, described in Exodus 13: 14 as "deliverance from the house of bondage by the strength of the hand of the LORD". It was fraught with hardship and difficulty, but the LORD went before Israel in a pillar of cloud to lead the way by day, and in a pillar of fire to give them light by night. His presence was constantly with them.

They were pursued by the Egyptians all the way to the Red Sea. With fear rising in their hearts, Israel cried out to the Lord, "We want to go back!" Moans and complaints spilled out of their hearts.

> "Didn't we say to you in Egypt, 'Leave us alone; let us serve the Egyptians'? It would have been better for us to serve the Egyptians than to die in the desert!" (Exodus 14: 12 NIV).

Moses instructed the people to stand still, to not be afraid, and to see the salvation of the Lord. God would vanquish the enemy; He would fight for them. Moses lifted his rod and stretched it over the Red Sea. The Lord caused a strong east wind to rise, and the waters miraculously divided. All Israel walked safely through on dry ground. God hardened the hearts of the Egyptians, and they pursued Israel into the Red Sea. The Lord threw them in confusion, causing their chariots to swerve and the wheels to come off. Then the Lord commanded Moses to stretch out his hand over the sea and the waters crashed down on the Egyptians – not one survived. And Israel feared and believed the LORD.

Egypt Was Still Ruling Their Hearts

As they reached the wilderness, unbelievably, they started moaning and groaning again. How could they, after all they had seen and experienced of Almighty God?! What were they thinking? Perhaps the answer is not hard to find: *Egypt was still ruling their hearts!* They had left Egypt, but Egypt had not left them. God had revealed His love, and they had witnessed the thrilling sight of being led by the cloud and the pillar of fire, the parting of the Red Sea, manna raining down from heaven, water gushing out of a rock, yet *their hearts were hard and remained unchanged.* No matter what God had done, their hearts wanted to go back to Egypt. When God tested Israel in the wilderness, what ruled and possessed their hearts spilled out. Years of brutal slavery, abuse, harsh treatment, hardship, rejection, and feelings of abandonment in Egypt had contributed to their aggressive, independent, unrestrained, angry, and self-sufficient hearts. This is a picture of the hardened pathway described by Jesus in the parable! Many believers are burdened with a past for which they have not received healing. Tragically, the body of Christ displays the resultant bitter fruit and ungodly behaviour.

Hebrews 3: 7–11 offers helpful commentary on what happened in the wilderness: "Therefore, as the Holy Spirit says: 'Today, if you will hear His voice, *do not harden your hearts as in the rebellion,* in the day of trial in the wilderness, where your fathers tested Me, tried Me, and saw My works forty years. Therefore I was angry with that generation, and said, 'They always go astray in their heart, and they have not known My ways.' So I swore in My wrath, 'They shall not enter My rest.''"" (NKJV, emphasis added)

> "For whom, having heard, rebelled? Indeed, was it not all who came out of Egypt, led by Moses? Now with whom was He angry forty years? Was it not with those who sinned, whose corpses fell in the wilderness? And to whom did He swear that they would not enter His rest, but to those who did not obey? So we see they could not enter in because of unbelief" (Hebrews 3: 16–18 ASV).

They Hardened Their Own Hearts

Let's note that "they hardened their own hearts"—they chose unbelief. Taking into account all they had endured and lived through, we may be tempted to excuse their attitude and behaviour. Likewise, in today's society people may use their difficult childhood to justify their ungodly behaviour. But God held the Israelites responsible for their choices even under extreme and traumatic oppression. In Egypt Israel had forsaken and forgotten the God of Abraham, Isaac, and Jacob; instead of hardship and pain moving their hearts towards dependence on God, thus keeping their hearts soft and yielded to Him, they turned away, trusting only themselves. Hardship gave birth to unbelief. Mercifully, God had not forgotten them; He was watching and listening all the time, longing to intervene.

What Does Rebellious Mean?

In recent days, we have become desensitised to the real meaning of rebellion. In the Bible the word rebellion is defined in the context of "covenant relationship" between God and Israel. Israel rebelled against God's covenant love.

In Scripture, God's relationship with Israel is likened to the covenant of marriage. God made promises and sealed His covenant with Israel in blood. It is eternal and can never be broken by Him. In covenant, God offered Himself—He would be, and supply, everything they would ever need: His name, protection, provision, and most importantly, His loving and attentive presence. This is no casual, absent or neglectful husband;

He is devoted, gentle, kind, tender, loving, and attentive to their every cry. Rebellion took place when they spurned God's name, His love, His care, His provision, and His protection. They were unfaithful and adulterous to the covenant relationship. They rebelled against God. It was not just a small matter of having a tantrum, letting off steam, or taking license to express themselves after being cooped up in Egypt. They forsook God's covenant love and chose self-love, self-provision and self-protection. They chose pride and it cost the majority their inheritance in the Promised Land.

Imagine how God must have felt when, having pledged Himself, Israel grumbled, complained, and wanted to forsake Him and go back to Egypt. His heart must have been heavy with grief. Their hearts were so hardened that they would not settle down into God's loving protection and provision; they preferred the "old life" of Egypt, enslaved and oppressed. They behaved as if there were no marriage covenant. That is rebellion and it fills every heart that has not dealt with the painful legacy of the slavery and oppression of "Egypt" (our "old life" before salvation). Hebrews warns believers to be careful because the same danger of forsaking covenant lurks among believers today.

> "Beware, brethren, lest there be in any of you an evil heart of unbelief in departing from the living God; but exhort one another daily, while it is called "Today," lest any of you be hardened through the deceitfulness of sin. For we have become partakers of Christ if we hold the beginning of our confidence steadfast to the end, while it is said: "Today, if you will hear His voice, do not harden your hearts as in the rebellion." (Hebrews 3: 12 NKJV).

2. The Children of Israel in the Promised Land

Let's compare the attitude of the children of Israel in the wilderness to the attitude of the children of Israel in the Promised Land. It was a different generation of the children of Israel, specifically Judah, and they were under threat of attack by their enemies.

Read 2 Chronicles 20: 1–30

This is a marvellous story of God's covenant faithfulness, Israel's belief and the resultant victory. Jehoshaphat, the king of Judah, feared as he faced *"a great multitude coming against him"* (2 Chronicles 20: 2, emphasis added)—who wouldn't? But in contrast to the children of Israel in the wilderness, his fear drove him to seek the Lord and to fast. "Then all Judah, with their little ones and wives, stood before the Lord" (2 Chronicles 20: 13 NKJV). The people followed the example of their leader. "Suddenly the Holy Spirit came upon Jahaziel, and He said, 'Listen, all of you, and you, King Jehoshaphat! Thus says the LORD to you: Do not be afraid or dismayed because of this great multitude, for the battle is not yours, but God's'" (2 Chronicles 20: 15) "You do not *need* to fight in this *battle.* Position yourselves, stand still, and see the salvation of the LORD, who is with you. Do not fear or be dismayed; tomorrow go out against them, for the LORD *is* with you" (2 Chronicles 20: 17 NKJV).

They Looked to their Covenant Partner

Where did faith focus its eye? It was certainly not on the great advancing army; otherwise, they would have been paralysed by intimidation. Their belief focussed on the One to whom they belonged and trusted. God's covenant love, character, and ability assured Judah of victory.

Jehoshaphat bowed his head with his face to the ground and worshipped. Then as a nation belonging to God, they acted on what God had said through the prophetic voice; they rose up and went out to face the enemy. Belief was an action, not just a notion. They fully engaged and cooperated with God in covenant partnership, He being the head, chief, and master. In covenant their enemies were His enemies; He would watch over them to bring victory. He would not leave them or forsake them. Belief laid hold of covenant promise!

As they moved out, Jehoshaphat exhorted them: "*Believe* in the LORD your God and you shall be established; *believe* His prophets, and you shall prosper" (2 Chronicles 20: 20, NKJV, emphasis added). As they stood still and took their position, they began to sing and praise the beauty of God's holiness, and the LORD set ambushes against their enemy.

The enemy was defeated! (2 Chronicles 20: 21) Can you imagine how they must have felt as they took hold of God's hand and let Him lead them to victory? They didn't stay at home nurturing a vision of victory, they took part; how their hearts must have brimmed with thankfulness, joy, and immense love. Then, like a doting husband, He said, "Go ahead, the spoils are yours". He blessed them with the spoils of His battle and filled them with joy, and the fear of the Lord gripped the surrounding nations as they heard what God had done and how He had done it (2 Chronicles 20: 29).

Their response stands in stark contrast to that of Israel in the wilderness. In the wilderness Israel responded in unbelief (rebellion); in the Promised Land they flourished in their trust and tenderness of heart towards God.

What is it to Believe?

These are marvellous stories, but they were not written to simply record history or to entertain the reader. They were written to shape our thoughts about "belief" and "unbelief" (rebellion). It says in 2 Chronicles 20:20, "*Believe in the LORD your God*" (NKJV, emphasis added). In discipleship we must answer the question:

- What does it mean to believe?

The word used here for "believe" is *aman,* defined in Strong's Dictionary as, "To be firm, stable, established; also, to be firmly persuaded or to believe solidly". In its causative form, *aman* means, "to consider trustworthy". The most famous derivative is the word which we use to conclude a prayer: "*amen*". Our loud "amen" declares, "Yes, we consider God faithful and trustworthy in what we have just committed to Him".

Aman is the word used in Genesis 15: 6 where God cut covenant with Abraham and all the nations, and in response Abraham declared that he "believed" in the Lord. His belief declared, "Yes, I consider God trustworthy in all that He has promised in covenant." Abraham had faith in God's faithfulness. On the basis of blood covenant Abraham believed that God would never break or rescind His promises. It was not head knowledge, Abraham *demonstrated* his *belief/faith* by every action that followed – he lived his life in covenant with God. Abraham knew the power, intent and certainty of what a blood covenant meant. Romans 11: 29 says, "Concerning the gospel they (Israel) are enemies for your sake, but concerning the election they are beloved for the sake of the fathers. For the gifts and the calling of God are irrevocable" (NKJV). That is the eternal strength and certainty of God's covenant with Israel and with us—irrevocable. We can stake our lives on it!

How Did Hardness of Heart Show Itself in the Wilderness?

Israel's hardness of heart in the wilderness was revealed in their unbelief (rebellion). They failed to "consider God trustworthy"; they failed "to be persuaded" or to "believe solidly" (Strong's Dictionary). They did not have faith in His faithfulness. They only saw God through the lens of their experience of the harsh and cruel ruler, Pharaoh, and were unwilling, or perhaps not yet able to believe who God was, His unconditional love, and His beneficial purpose. They refused to trust His faithful and loving-kindness; they preferred to take their chances back in Egypt. Their attitude and actions exposed their hardness of heart. "Happy is the man who is always reverent, but he who hardens his heart will fall into calamity" (Proverbs 28: 14 NKJV).

Over time, wilful and prolonged rebellion against God, His sovereignty and healing love will surely harden our hearts. Without repentance it will come to a point where we are unable to sense God's presence, let alone hear His voice. This hardening *process* can begin with something small, perhaps a disappointment in church or being let down by a friend. We may have been wronged, or we may have wronged someone else. It may be something more grave and devastating, like the betrayal of a spouse, injustice, or a tragic personal loss that seeds bitterness, jealousy, and revenge in our heart. These are things we may face in life. The outcome of such situations is determined by the decision we make:

- Do we forgive and turn in dependence towards God?
- Do we allow Him to handle our battles or do we take matters into our own hands?
- Are we guilty of allowing the legacy of wounding and pain to stack up like a wall of unbelief against God?

The hardened heart has a strong independent spirit, so the response to attack or challenge is usually hostile, pushing everyone away, and toughing it out alone. The hardened heart prefers to control its own life. It venomously attacks to defend.

Deal With Hardness of Heart

Let's open our heart and repent of all rebellion that rejects God's covenant love for us. God's loving-kindness invites us to come for healing. For too many, the broken past has left a legacy of hardness of heart. Let's not be deceived into believing that "not dealing with it" is, in fact, "dealing with it". We have only to ask victims of abuse if "letting it be" has changed anything. Putting our head in the sand usually means the problem is buried or suppressed, not solved or healed. We can't even say we have hidden it from sight because the longer we leave it festering, the harder of heart we become. Unhealthy and harmful reactions will manifest every time a situation similar to the one in which we were wounded turns up. Hardness of heart is surprisingly easy to recognise because it betrays itself through sarcasm, cynicism, outbursts of anger, and intimidating behaviour. To be around hardened people is difficult; we have to tread on eggshells and learn to duck. God longs to break the destructive cycles of our past; Jesus came to set the prisoner free.

Summary: Causes of Hardness of Heart

- Cumulative and unresolved wounding and pain
- Forgetting, neglecting, or ignoring God
- Independence from God
- Spiritual adultery – choosing to place your trust in something or someone other than God
- Unforgiveness
- Habitual self-centredness; self is the idol

A Hardened Heart is Revealed by:

- Unbelief
- Unrestrained anger
- Suspicion, not easily persuaded, difficult, cynical
- Accusation, blaming others, never your fault
- Harshness
- Aggression and a challenging spirit
- Criticism
- Self-centredness and selfishness
- No reverence for God; disrespectful and dishonouring
- No repentance

Do you recognise any of these symptoms in your own life? Tick off any that define your heart or life.

The Tender Heart:

- Lives in the goodness of God's covenant love, protection, and provision
- Lives in communion with God
- Lives a lifestyle of worship
- Surrenders – it bows before God
- Lives in the reverential fear of the Lord

A Tender Heart is Revealed in:

- Belief
- Holiness
- Love for God's voice

- Watchfulness
- Readiness
- Trust
- Obedience to the Word of God
- Cooperation with God's plans

Do you recognise any of these symptoms in your own life? Tick off any that define your heart or life.

What Hope Is There for Such a Condition of Heart?

Our hope is always God's mercy, long-suffering, and tenacious love. It is the mercy of God that "takes us around the mountain again", often repeating challenging circumstances and experiences to chisel away at the hardness in our hearts. Does God plan to punish or hurt us through that process? No, He simply wants to get our attention and deliver us from the evil that is eating us up from the inside. He longs that we turn back into His loving arms, embracing the full blessing of covenant relationship again. He waits for us to repent.

How the heart of our Father in heaven must weep over hardness in the heart of His children. How grieved He must be when we prefer bitterness and resentment, not even considering bringing our pain, sorrow, and wounds to Him for healing. Mercifully, time and again, God steps in before we hit the self-destruct button. If we will not be trained and instructed by the Word of God, He will faithfully provide other loving training methods, such as famine, storms, exile, and adverse conditions to appeal to our hearts to return to Him. God never wastes our sorrows.

He offered us immense love, freedom, healing, and restoration at the cross. Doesn't it seem a little foolish that we should refuse all that the blood of Jesus, shed on the cross, represents and offers? The great South African writer, teacher, and Christian pastor Andrew Murray once said, "What would have happened if the children of Israel had only placed the blood of the lamb in a bowl by the door of their home, instead of applying it to their doorposts? They would have been destroyed". We must *apply* the blood, not simply *believe in* the blood! If we refuse or neglect to *apply* the healing and cleansing power of the blood of Jesus, we are, in effect, saying Jesus' blood is not enough to deal with what ails us. By refusing to forgive or to be forgiven, hardening our heart to God's loving and tender love, we are really saying that we do not need Him; we can work it out on our own. That is rebellion and unbelief.

We can be thankful that, just like the farmer, God continues to faithfully sow, even on the hardened pathway, longing for a harvest of blessing in the lives of each of His precious and beloved children. This is God's covenant love that will never let us go.

A Selah Moment

No doubt we need a long pause after reading this chapter; it is deeply challenging. First, let's pray.

Prayer

"Lord, show me my heart. Are there any areas of hardness not receptive to Your seed? Please sift back through the archives of my life to see if at any point I spurned Your love and care, choosing to do things my way, suppressing pain, and holding on to anger. When did I forsake the cross and refuse to apply Your blood? Lord, show me symptoms of hardness in my life; any reactions I have that reveal anger and defensiveness. Show me what causes me to be sarcastic and cynical. Help me to recognise when experiences or storms come in cycles, through which You want to get my attention, uncovering unhealthy and harmful attitudes and behaviour that need repentance and deliverance. Lord, thank You that in Your love and mercy You will lead me through a thorough examination, washing, cleansing, delivering and restoring me. I long for a deep work of grace in my life. I want to be tender of heart towards You and others. Amen".

Make it a matter of intentional prayer this week to ask the Holy Spirit to put His finger on areas of hardness in your heart. If you find yourself saying, "I don't want to go there", write in your journal what it is that you remember, and the feelings that are being stirred. It will be beneficial to share these things with your life group, requesting their prayer support.

This deeper level of discipleship requires courage, but it is essential for spiritual growth and fruitfulness.

Questions to Consider and Answer

- How does "belief" or "faith" manifest in your life? Recall situations where you turned your eyes away from the "strength of the enemy" as did Jehoshaphat, to focus on God's character and ability to bring you through to victory. Journal your thoughts.
- How does "unbelief" manifest in your life? As you read this chapter, what responses were triggered? What situation(s) did your mind recall? Things long-hidden and suppressed may have surfaced. Where and when did you take your life into your own hands, not bringing your need to the Lord? It is important to list these in your journal because it is time to clear the old ground for new growth.

Life Group

This week life group moves to yet a deeper level of trust as you uncover things in your heart that you wish were not there. This is exactly the point where Satan would want to hold you back in shame, and where God wants you to move forward into His light where darkness is dispelled, and joy fills your heart.

Before you begin, let each one verbalise again their commitment to practise love, acceptance, understanding, and confidentiality within the group. Des, my late husband, used to say, "Jan, you know I love you". And I would answer, "Yes, but I love hearing you say it". Many need this kind of audible embrace and reassurance.

Let it be stressed again that you are not each other's counsellor; you are a loyal and relational support group. For some, just having the opportunity to express honestly will start to break up hardened ground in the heart, and for others it may take more time. Don't try to force growth; the Holy Spirit will promote growth as your willingness grows.

Be attentive, reassuring, interested, and compassionate in the group. God is our Redeemer; nothing is too *hard* for Him!

Use the following questions to stimulate honest sharing:

- What part of Chapter 6 spoke specifically to you? What is your response? What feelings have surfaced?
- Describe how tenderness of heart towards God has developed in you. What evidence of tenderness is visible?
- What areas of "hardness of heart" has God put His finger on?

Give time for each one to share. Please be honest with each other; your honesty may bring healing to someone else in the group. Many times what one shares releases honesty in another.

Leave thirty minutes for prayer. This week pray *for yourself.* You may want to bring to the Lord specific areas of your life, you may need to confess sin, or you may simply want to yield your life afresh to Jesus Christ. Even though it is hard, be specific and verbalise your feelings to the Lord. Allow people to weep in brokenness without cushioning what God is doing. As each prays, pray for him or her.

At the end of the book you will find "The Gift of Forgiveness" (A lesson from *The Lifestyle of the Disciple*) published here with the kind permission of my dear friends Reuven and Yanit Ross (Making Disciples International—see Appendix). No matter what your story, it will inevitably lead you to the cross to seek forgiveness for yourself, or to extend forgiveness to those who have caused wounding and emotional pain. This lesson will instruct and help you in how to forgive.

You may need to spend another week in Chapter 6 to allow people to thoroughly share their hardness of heart. It is a discipleship season, so take time. Don't rush.

Your group may choose to spend the following week on the "The Gift of Forgiveness" and practise the prescribed "pattern for forgiving others". Allow flexibility in your schedule. Be led by the Holy Spirit.

Scriptures for Meditation

"And the LORD your God will circumcise your heart and the heart of your descendants, to love the LORD your God with all your heart and with all your soul that you may live" (Deuteronomy 30: 6 NKJV).

"For he is not a Jew who is one outwardly, nor is circumcision that which is outward in the flesh; but he is a Jew who is one inwardly; and circumcision is that of the heart , in the Spirit, not in the letter; whose praise is not from men but from God" (Romans 2: 28–29 NKJV).

CHAPTER 7:

Rocks Galore

Read Mark 4: 5 and Mark 4: 16

> "Some fell on stony ground, where it did not have much earth; and immediately it sprang up because it had no depth of earth. But when the sun was up it was scorched, and because it had no root it withered away" (Mark 4: 5 NKJV).
>
> "These likewise are the ones sown on stony ground who, when they hear the word, immediately they hear it with gladness; and they have no root in themselves, and so only endure for a time. Afterward, when tribulation or persecution arises for the word's sake, immediately they stumble" (Mark 4: 16 NKJV).

According to Jesus, those with rocks in their hearts hear God's Word just like everyone else, but the impact of His Word is short-lived. Jesus tells us this soil is characterised by its shallowness. There is no depth for God's seed to bed and form strong roots. Therefore, when God's Word is sown into this heart, it can only ever achieve a tiny fraction of its potential. Let's remind ourselves again, there is nothing wrong with God's seed; the problem lies with what else the soil contains. Hidden rocks cause the soil to be shallow and unproductive. The seed sprouts and quickly pushes up through the shallow soil; however, with no root to feed on, it soon withers in the scorching sun. There is no lasting growth, and fruit is never seen!

This believer gets excited about powerful messages or sermons, but seems tragically unaffected and unchanged by what is heard. Come Monday morning, in a spiritually unsympathetic world, they blend into their surroundings, speaking and acting like everyone else. Their behaviour does not distinguish them from their ungodly colleagues. The enthusiastic response to the powerful message evaporates in the wind. The soil of this believer's heart is so shallow that when trouble and persecution arise because of the Word of God, they stumble. Evidently, these are believers who tend to blow hot and cold, but what in their hearts causes this?

Jesus does not hide the fact that trouble and persecution *will come because of the Word*. It is the rootedness of the Word of God in our hearts that will be tested. In the Beatitudes, Jesus said, *"Blessed are those who are persecuted for righteousness' sake, for theirs is the kingdom of heaven"* (Matthew 5: 10, NKJV, emphasis added). Trouble and persecution are the guaranteed "side-effects" of planting God's righteous seed, about which we are clearly warned on the seed package! Because God's seed is righteous *it* will call and direct from within to live righteously. But, for those who are shallow spiritually, the power and goodness of God's seed has little effect. They are weak and ineffective believers. The rocks in their hearts dictate and determine a superficial spiritual life. Under fire, when it matters, they do not stand up for what is right. They stumble.

Why Does the Word of God Attract Persecution?

It is God who defines and declares what righteousness is, it is not for man to decide what is right. We need to understand that the same Word that brings light and robust faith in our hearts also exposes darkness and unbelief in others. People don't take kindly to their darkness being exposed, so they single out believers who hold fast to the Word of God to discredit and belittle. There are many examples.

Today, if we dare stand up for God's standard of sexual purity, even in the body of Christ, we may find *we* are "disciplined" instead of those living in immorality. We will be discriminated against for being true to God's Word. This is persecution for righteousness' sake. To walk in humility is righteousness. Humble attitudes and behaviour expose those who are full of themselves. Those walking in pride retaliate with bullying, accusing the humble of what they themselves are guilty of. They seek to keep the upper hand through intimidation, maltreatment and excessive control. People in pride cause trouble for humble believers.

If we stand up for honesty and transparency in the workplace in time-keeping or the completion of tax forms, we are likely to be hounded by unscrupulous colleagues. Integrity is righteousness and it is hated by those who operate in the shadows of dishonesty and lies. The light and truth of God's Word will always provoke an angry and venomous response from those who love darkness. Being truthful is living righteously. Proverbs 11: 1 says, "Dishonest scales are an abomination to the LORD, but a just weight is His delight" (NKJV).

It says in Genesis 1: 27–28, "So God created man in His own image; in the image of God He created him; male and female He created them. Then God blessed them, and God said to them, "be fruitful and multiply" (NKJV). Genesis 2: 24 says, "Therefore a man shall leave his father and mother and be joined to his wife, and they shall become one flesh" (NKJV). God's righteous Word defines marriage as the union of man and woman. To uphold that truth will mean a fierce battle with the spirit of the world. To be actively "pro-life", standing true to God's commandment, "You shall not kill", will mean facing a strong tide of abuse and intimidating threats from those who believe in abortion and euthanasia. Shallow believers will either avoid all such contention and controversy or "sit on the fence" compromising God's truth. They cannot speak up for God's character and His righteous and loving ways because the Word of God has not been able to root in them. They falter and fall.

In the interest of "tolerance" we will be increasingly pressured to call good evil, and evil good, and tribulation and persecution will find out whether God's Word is truly the plumb line of our hearts. Our resolve to only please the Lord will be tested, and it will cost dearly. However, let's rejoice because we have a great reward in heaven! (Matthew 5: 10) We have to decide. If the presence of rocks causes the soil of our hearts to be shallow, we need humility, courage, and determination to ask Jesus to identify, break them down, or remove them! Surely we do not want to live the rest of our days as a shallow believer, up and down with seasonal enthusiasm? Our wonderful God wants far more than that for us; He longs for a deeply joyful, unfettered, and intimate union with us. All believers must take a confident stand for truth whatever the personal cost. This is what it means to fellowship in the sufferings of Christ Jesus. He gives us the grace and power to endure and overcome.

Philippians 3: 7–11 says, "But what things were gain to me, these I have counted loss for Christ. Yet indeed I also count all things loss for the excellence of the knowledge of Christ Jesus my Lord, for whom I have suffered the loss of all things, and count them as rubbish, that I may gain Christ and be found in Him, not having my own righteousness, which is from the law, but that which is through faith in Christ, the righteousness which is from God by faith; that I may know Him and the power of His resurrection, and the fellowship of His sufferings , being conformed to His death, if, by any means, I may attain to the resurrection from the dead" (NKJV).

How are Rocks Formed?

In geological terms, rocks are a small or large mixture of minerals layered and compacted. This is a helpful picture of what Jesus was alluding to. What can layer and compact in our lives to form such negative, hard, and impenetrable rocklike formations?

Let's consider the effect of old and painful hurts and wounds that have never been brought to Jesus for healing. Many of us share a common history of being deeply hurt in our formative years – some unspeakably so. We experienced rejection. Family life may have been tough and dysfunctional; the love, attention, encouragement, and acceptance we needed never materialised. We may have been mocked because some thought we were too fat, too skinny, too tall, or too small. We may have been ridiculed because we were said to be less attractive or less intelligent. We may have been verbally or physically abused by a member of our family. We may have been bereaved, abandoned, or orphaned. We may have experienced or suffered a painful loss – perhaps by being moved away from close and valued friends with whom we felt safe and secure. We may have been overlooked and put down while our sibling was treated as special. Whatever it was, not yet knowing there was a healing Saviour to whom we could run and in whom we could shelter, we buried our pain deep in our soul. Life may have moved on, but the devastating effects of early wounding can live on in our souls into adulthood and manifest in the way we respond or react to God, ourselves, and other people.

Rejection Can Form Rocks

Rejection forms the foundation layer of many troublesome rocks. It can lead to the layering of unresolved and unhealed pain, resentment, bitterness and unbelief (rebellion). At this stage a person cannot believe God is loving and faithful because memories and experiences testify to something entirely different. We may not be completely hardened as in the first soil, but we have clusters of rocklike sinful attitudes and behaviour.

Some deeply hurt people become ambitious and driven; they don't mind whom they step on to get to the top. Others become abusive and angry. Others constantly seek approval and recognition at home, socially, or at work. They feel the need to prove themselves and often have a critical spirit. Others adopt a well-screened independent lifestyle where nobody can come close. They have no need of others. Others seem to always press and test the limits of relationships in their insecurity – they are difficult friends to have around: argumentative, aggressive, and antagonistic. Others slip into their shell of self-pity – life for them is full of moans and groans; their cup is always half-empty. Others seek love and acceptance by offering themselves cheaply in inappropriate relationships, sadly compounding and reinforcing their sense of worthlessness. Others turn to addictions – to sex, food, personal image or appearance, pornography, drugs, gambling, smoking, alcohol, shopping, or money – to cope with their pain.

God Weeps While Satan Laughs

Unresolved and unhealed pain seeks love, approval, recognition, and acceptance in all the wrong places, and with all the wrong people. Why do we burst out in aggressive anger under certain circumstances? Why do we block out or react negatively to people? Why do we have difficulty accepting that God is love? Why do we hold on to our money with a tight fist criticising others who are in need? Why do we flirt around the opposite sex, selling ourselves cheaply and seeking attention? We may never have connected our hardened and sinful attitudes and behaviour with yesterday's painful events, but it is time to take responsibility before God for how we have responded. God knows and does not abandon us. His Spirit, the Spirit of grace, convicts of sin and walks us repentantly to the cross where God's love and forgiveness flows incessantly like a crystal and pure river. God can and will heal past wounds, hurt, and pain by the power of the blood of His Son Jesus Christ when we humbly submit our suffering to His healing hand.

God weeps for such brokenness. It is not how He intends life to be. He desires that every child be unconditionally loved, unreservedly accepted, immeasurably encouraged, honourably recognised, and fully appreciated. Wounds need healing. This is why He sent His only Son, Jesus, to this earth. In His love He wanted to reconnect us to the Source of wholeness in body, soul and spirit.

Of course Satan wants to keep everyone from healing and reconciliation with God! He crouches behind the powerful messages of rejection and worthlessness, meticulously layering lie upon lie into our belief system, forming rocks in our soul that ultimately cultivate unbelief and deny place to the seed of God's Word. He sows lies about God, about us, and about others. They hold us captive to unbelief about the true character of God.

We All Are Vulnerable

Whatever age or whatever sex, we are all vulnerable to the formation of troublesome rocks – "a small or large mixture of minerals layered and compacted together". It can happen at any stage of our lives when we do not handle the hurts, disappointments, and tragedies of life in God's way. Rather than allowing God to break down the rocks, we are arrogant, thinking we can somehow work our spiritual lives around them. However, that is impossible without serious implications! We must come to an understanding of how sin operates to form rocks in our lives!

Permitted, consistent and excused sinful patterns layer and compact in our hearts, forming hardened attitudes and strongholds that prevent and resist spiritual growth. Rocks are like strongholds and they must be cast down, because they exalt themselves against the knowledge of God. They imprison us in unbelief.

Read 2 Corinthians 10: 4–6: "For the weapons of our warfare are not carnal but mighty in God for pulling down strongholds, casting down arguments and every high thing that exalts itself against the knowledge of God, bringing every thought into captivity to the obedience of Christ, and being ready to punish all disobedience when your obedience is fulfilled" (NKJV).

Read Proverbs 21: 22; it also gives us some good godly counsel: "A wise man scales the city of the mighty and brings down the trusted stronghold" (NKJV).

If we truly desire growth and if that is the sincere cry of our heart to God in prayer, the Holy Spirit will faithfully expose the rocks that hinder the reception of God's love and prevent spiritual growth. His way is quite simple – come humbly to Jesus, rolling all hurt, pain, and shame onto Him. He has already identified with our suffering and carried each experience to the cross. If, however, we choose to bury injustices and their effect, choosing rather to "turn a blind eye", or put up with their consequences, we must realise we are leaving the door open for Satan to layer the consequences of pain and suffering in the soil of our hearts. We will struggle. Rocks resistant and impervious to the power of God's Word will form. They will bed in our heart even more deeply, and the rope of captivity will tighten like a noose. Make no mistake, we are prisoners to old works of the flesh and painful events from the past if they still control us. It will be impossible for God's seed to find any depth of soil.

According to the Word of God, all works of the flesh are symptomatic of some sort of rebellion and unbelief in the heart.

Read Galatians 5: 19–21

> "Now the works of the flesh are evident, which are: adultery, fornication, uncleanness, lewdness, idolatry, sorcery, hatred,

contentions, jealousies, outbursts of wrath, selfish ambitions, dissensions, heresies, envy, murders, drunkenness, revelries, and the like; of which I tell you beforehand, just as I also told you in time past, that those who practice such things will not inherit the kingdom of God" (NKJV).

Galatians 6: 7–10 goes on to say, "Do not be deceived, God is not mocked; for whatever a man sows, that he will also reap. For he who sows to his flesh will of the flesh reap corruption, but he who sows to the Spirit will of the Spirit reap everlasting life. And let us not grow weary while doing good, for in due season we shall reap if we do not lose heart" (NKJV).

What Hope is There for a Rocky Heart?

This chapter poses a major challenge to the body of Christ. More than enough seed is being sown, but so little of it is able to take root because of the rocks so easily accommodated in the hearts of believers. Great damage is caused by the presence of rocks, whether we are aware of them or not. Their presence means that we are missing out on the glories of the kingdom of God. God wants to help us break down the rocks in our hearts so His seed will root and flourish.

Is there hope for a rocky heart? Yes, there is always hope for the one who humbles himself sincerely before the Lord and asks for His help. All we need to pray is, "Lord, help me. What are the rocks in my life that hinder the productivity of your seed-Word taking root in my heart and producing a harvest?" God delights in answering this prayer; however, be prepared, because the answer requires death of your flesh and that you pick up and carry your cross! Prepare for upheaval and pressure as God begins the process of breaking down or removing offending rocks. The spiritual reward of an open, close relationship with the Lord is worth all the effort!

How are Rocks Broken Down?

According to Wikipedia.com, http://wiki.answers.com/Q/What_breaks_rocks_into_gravel_sand_or_soil: "It is *erosion* that breaks rocks into gravel, sand, and soil" (emphasis added).

- Wind drives rain or dust or sand into rocks and this abrades them, wearing them away.
- Water can wash over rocks and wear them away, or it can carry sediment (fine bits of dirt or sand) which can abrade them and wear them down.
- Water can rush at rocks and pound them in a torrent, lifting them and smashing them into each other as in a flood.
- Water can slip into tiny cracks in rock and freeze there, breaking off bits of the rock itself (due to ice expanding as the water it is created from, freezes).

Certainly any catastrophic geologic event can cause massive changes in large rock formations, shifting countless tons of rock and pounding them against each other. Glaciers can grind rocks to dust. "'Is not my word like a fire?' says the LORD, 'and like a hammer that breaks the rock in pieces?'" (Jeremiah 23: 29).

The erosion of rocks resembles invasive, overwhelming, stressful, and painful events that God, in His loving faithfulness, uses to prepare our hearts for His seed to effect the experience of salvation. Let's allow the driving wind of the Holy Spirit, and the pounding water of God's Word, to do their loving work in our hearts. It may take time, but eventually the rocks will be ground down to minerals to enrich the soil of our hearts. God turns what Satan meant for evil into good!

A True Story: The Enemy Meant it for Harm; God Meant it for Good

A nine-year-old child named John lived next door. He was a little scallywag – the smallest of his gang of friends, with a mouth like a sewer and the manners of a spoilt brat. He irritated me no end.

We (Mintie and I) were returning from a two-month encouragement trip in our campervan, during which we had supported and served missionaries in Eastern Europe. We were full of joy and looking forward to getting home. As we eagerly turned the corner on to our street, we saw John and his gang of friends emerging from our back garden through a gap where a panel of fence used to be! They had removed and destroyed it. My heart raced, and blood surged to my head. Leaping from the van, I furiously chased John behind the garage compound, cornering him against the wall. I was breathing fire. Repressed anger erupted; my heart was seething, and I was in danger of losing control. A hand lightly brushed my shoulder; Mintie was gently trying to calm me. Inside my head I heard the insistent appeal, "Let it go!" I came to my senses and stepped back. John ran off to tell his mother, a smirk on his face. She soon appeared on our doorstep, threatening to call the police. "How could you have threatened my child?" she unjustly protested. She did not realise he was fortunate to be able to run home at all!

The sense of violation deepened as we surveyed our garden. We found damage to other pieces of fencing and plants that had been deliberately trampled. During the following weeks, mud and stones pelted our windows, and intimidating threats were shouted through the letterbox on the front door. We lived in fear, and the police seemed powerless and reluctant to intervene.

It was easy enough to justify my anger. I was within my rights to feel aggrieved; it was normal. After all, John and his friends had caused criminal damage. But deep in my heart I knew God was taking me through a deeper lesson of discipleship; the tribulation and persecution of the children uncovered strongholds of anger and fear in my heart. I realised my reaction to John was inordinate to the situation; he was a naughty and unsupervised boy, but not a criminal worthy of the death penalty!

If I had let myself bask in the pride of self-justification I would have been left with impenetrable rocks and shallowness of soil that would have prevented growth. I would not have understood God's loving message: "Jan, it is time to get you out of the prison of anger and fear". I needed to come to the place where I humbled myself to ask, "Lord, what are You trying to teach me in this?"

The weeks passed and instead of things getting better, they got worse. I was shaken as pressure mounted. The Automobile Association took a double payment from my bank account, and what seemed like an easy and honourable customer-service decision to repay the instalment became a prolonged saga of having to prove *their* wrongdoing. I got the "bit between my teeth" and anger bubbled over like lava; every now and again the volcano spat out ash!

Then we had a new blind fitted at home. The company sent a "young buck" to install it. From the outset he was cocky and would not be advised. He finished the job and promptly, without hesitation, held out his hand for payment. When I later went to admire the new blind, I noticed there was a deep scratch down the wall just under the hole he had drilled for a screw. Of course it hadn't been there when he came, but he would not accept responsibility. I entered into another battle! For months I smoked and fumed, trying to get the firm to come and repair the damage, or at least offer some form of compensation, but to no avail.

I might not have taken notice of these experiences in isolation, but God helpfully clustered them to help me realise I had a deeper problem than just a fence, a double payment, or a scratch on the wall. By this time, I was so deeply rattled I had become unreasonable. I should have been able to maturely confront each of my offenders with gentleness of spirit; instead, I exploded into symptomatic aggressive and sinful behaviour. I was prisoner to rebellion and unbelief. With a little help from the Holy Spirit, and Mintie, the "penny dropped", and light began to dawn. Mintie tried so carefully to choose words that would help me become aware of my less-than-helpful aggressive attitudes; then she ducked!

On reflection, I realise God, in His love, was saying, "That is enough; it is time to heal my Jan. She is destroying herself!" He lovingly exposed the rocks of anger and fear. It was evident they were hampering my spiritual progress.

Desperation compelled me to withdraw from people and circumstances, to earnestly seek the Lord. I will remember forever the sheer relief I experienced as I fell to my knees and poured out the pain of years of injustice and abuse. Even though it is true that most of the "rocks" in my heart had been formed by events beyond my control, I was still responsible for my responses and the subsequent building of the walls of unbelief and rebellion around my heart. Revisiting long-buried and painful memories was excruciating, but the depth of pain was more than matched by Jesus' comfort and healing. As the complex layers of pain oozed out their poison, Jesus gathered me into His loving and merciful arms and held me tight. I broke.

I had been utterly exposed but was entirely safe because God had exposed the rocks for the sake of deliverance, healing, and love, not to abuse and control. In the privacy of that special retreat with my Lord, a deeper understanding of God's love was seeded in my fragile heart. A deep and honest repentance gave birth to life in the Holy Spirit. I had been delivered of fear and anger as the rocks and debris of many years had been removed. I experienced significant changes in my walk with the Lord. I knew for the very first time in my Christian walk what it meant to offer a broken and contrite heart as a sacrifice to the Lord (Psalm 51: 17). It created in me a deep love for God's voice and His daily presence, from which I have never looked back. I noticed a new ability to receive revelation from the Word of God; I felt "tuned in and tuned up". I sensed I was spiritually alert – not only for my sake, but to help others.

I am so thankful to the Lord for John, the AA man, and the fitter of the blinds! The enemy meant all those experiences for harm, but God meant them for good (Genesis 50: 20).

Some Loving Advice

- Train and discipline yourself to regularly invite God to examine your heart. Know for certain God does not want to harm you, even if He needs a hammer to pulverise a rock.
- Choose the path of humility, and allow close friends to help you identify strongholds in your heart.
- Learn to see "rocks" as the enemy of growth and His exposure and removal of them as love. He purposes to cleanse your heart, clear the contaminated soil, and bless you with divine growth and fruitfulness.
- Learn to "flag up" repetitive behavioural or mood cycles. Have you reacted like that before?
    - When you recognise that you are habitually going round the same mountain, urgently and intentionally seek the Lord. Ask, "Lord, what are You teaching me?"

- When you feel a distance between you and the Lord, ask, "Lord, what hinders our relationship?" He will answer you. Be alert to the sequence of events that follows your prayer!
- When you feel a distance between you and a brother or sister in the Lord, ask the same question, "Lord, what hinders our relationship?" He will show you.

The Most Common Rock: Offence – 1 Peter 2: 1–10

I cannot close this chapter without drawing attention to the rock of offence; it is common to all our hearts and has incredible power to manipulate and destroy believers and fellowship. "An offended brother is more unyielding than a fortified city, and disputes are like barred gates of a citadel" (Proverbs 18: 19 NKJV). Other Scriptures you can read are Proverbs 11: 13, 12: 18, 12: 23, 18: 8, 19: 11; and Leviticus 19: 16.

The Greek word for "offence" is *skandalon,* from which we get the word "scandal". A skandalon was a movable stick that triggered a trap. When an animal touched or bit the stick, the trap would fall on it, snaring the creature.

When we take offence, we are scandalised. Jesus says we're not to be offended and we are not to pick up on the offences of others. That is not easy to do – somehow offence has magnetic attraction! There is nothing like a good piece of gossip to get your teeth into, right? A group of gossipers seem far more animated than a group discussing Sunday's sermon! Our flesh is so easily drawn into the trap; our interest is aroused, and we inquisitively brush the stick, springing the trap. We are suddenly trapped in a web of gossip and controversy, which inevitably leads to sinful thoughts and hurtful actions, regardless of who was right or wrong.

Gossipers retain just a portion of what they heard and broadcast it as though it were the whole picture. The case against the poor victim is airtight. Partakers in gossip, who have a particular axe to grind, apply a filter to what they hear, retaining what is useful, "to confirm what they had thought all along", thus making their own so-called legitimate case against the person being scandalised.

Gossip is usually characterised by an unwillingness to go to the one being talked about to hear his or her side of the story. In Christian circles it is often deceitfully disguised by saying, "I'm just sharing this with you for prayer", or "I think you ought to know about this; I only have their best interest at heart". Lives are damaged and reputations shredded by exaggeration, misunderstanding, and malice; the evil of gossip spreads like wildfire. This is not a game or something trivial; it is evil.

We have the capacity to both offend and be offended. If not dealt with at the cross as they arise, these offences eventually become bitter and twisted strongholds of Satan. An offended heart is strongly resistant to spiritual growth because it is consumed by its self-righteousness.

Repentance is mandatory. Gossip is a sin. It needs to be confessed to the Lord and to the hearers of your gossip so healing may come (James 5: 16). The damage caused by gossip is immense as it is not a victimless sin. We harm our brothers and sisters with our unbridled tongue (Hebrews 12: 14–15), and we drive a wedge between God's heart and ours.

How to Deal with a Fellow Believer Who has Sinned Against You

Matthew 18: 15 gives clear instruction on disciplining an erring brother or sister (also see 1 Corinthians 5: 1–5; 1 Peter 2: 1–10; and Galatians 6: 1). Three progressive steps are specified as:

1. In private

2. In the presence of witnesses

3. If steps one and two have failed, tell the church.

We tend to impulsively neglect going to a person in private before speaking to others. But let's follow God's way. If we hear something negative about someone else, honour and respect the accused person by going to him or her first, in private. Love will always seek to cover and protect; love never rushes to the pastor or takes a megaphone and broadcasts sin to a group or the whole community. Talking with the person in private usually clears up most matters. Many situations arise due to misunderstandings, which, in private, can be calmly explained and understood.

We must humble ourselves before God and each other in this serious matter, forgiving and being forgiven. Jesus took the punishment for the sin of gossip. He offers pardon for confessed sin and cleansing from its stain. There are two sides to this coin: *the gossiper* is offered pardon and cleansing from the sin of slander, and *the one who was gossiped about* is cleansed from the shame that was laid on him or her. To leave a brother or sister floundering in the poison of gossip and scandal is to leave him or her isolated from fellowship. True pastoral care within the body of Christ needs to attend to wounds with great concern and love.

A Selah Moment

Let's pause – there's a lot to think about!

Prayer

"Lord, examine my heart; show me what rocks I should pay attention to. What rocks hinder spiritual growth? Is my heart contaminated? Is my heart proud? Holy Spirit sift through the soil of my heart because I long to be set free from what holds me captive and be filled with the life of Your Word. Lord, wash and thoroughly cleanse my heart. Draw me close to You. Amen".

Questions to Consider and Answer

This chapter asks some difficult, uncomfortable, but necessary questions.

Our negative attitudes and behaviours are symptomatic of the presence of rocks in our heart. The following list of symptoms may help you identify a rock or two hidden beneath the soil. Mark those applicable to you.

- Fear
- Anger

- Criticism
- Cynicism
- Aggression
- Unforgiveness
- Defensiveness
- Discontent
- Possessiveness
- Carnality
- Materialism
- Laziness
- Resentment
- Hatred
- Bitterness
- Moodiness
- Blame and finger-pointing
- Harshness
- Offence
- Addictions
- A loose tongue/gossip
- Stinginess
- Immoral activity
- Ungodly and forbidden sexual alliances

Just identifying symptoms may well stir memories of painful and wounding experiences that over time have compounded into a rock in your heart. You may now want to focus on one rocky area of your heart;

remember, the Holy Spirit is always your helper. The Holy Spirit is patient and will lead you one rock at a time. Be wise – do not attempt to deal with all the rocks at once.

Remember, rocks can be strongholds that take control of your attitudes and behaviour. They cause you to habitually sin. Take undivided time this week to pray, "Lord, what are You teaching me?"; "Lord, what hinders our relationship?"

Life Group

You will see that life group is becoming more and more essential in terms of having a safe and secure place to not only share but experience love and understanding. This chapter may have raised some serious concerns or touched some painful memories that need healing.

- First, invite the Holy Spirit to lead the group; you will need His help.
- Allow each one to share his or her answers to the questions about rocks in his or her heart.
    - Some may mention things without detail; others may welcome the opportunity to share "their story". The group needs to give time and space, allowing the Holy Spirit to move in hearts.
    - After each one has shared, allow opportunity for prayer, during which thoughts, feelings, and desires of the heart are expressed. Then allow people in the group to pray for others. This process may take some time.

What Do You Do With Identified Rocks?

Once again, at the end of the book you will find "The Gift of Forgiveness" (see Appendix). This will guide you through the process of repentance and forgiveness. No matter what your story is, it will inevitably lead you to the cross to seek forgiveness for yourself, or to extend forgiveness to those who have wounded you and caused you emotional pain.

Because of the depth of this chapter, your group may feel the need to spend another week on Chapter 7. It is a season for discipleship, so give each one the time he or she needs. Don't rush. Your group may also choose to spend one week on "The Gift of Forgiveness" and use the prescribed "pattern for forgiving others" in the following life group. Be flexible and allow the Holy Spirit to lead you.

Scripture for Meditation

> "If You, LORD, should mark iniquities, O Lord, who could stand? But there is forgiveness with You, that You may be feared. I wait for the LORD, my soul waits, and in His word I do hope. My soul waits for the Lord more than those who watch for the morning – yes, more than those who watch for the morning" (Psalm 130: 3–6 NKJV).

CHAPTER 8:

The Deadly Competition of Thorns

Introduction

We now look at the effect of thorns in a heart that desires growth. Throughout the Bible, thorns have a negative connotation, yet it is thought-provoking to note how thorns played a significant and sequential role in the unfolding drama of redemption.

1. First, thorns and thistles were not part of God's original creation (Genesis 3: 18). They came about as a consequence of sin when God punished Adam for his disobedience. God cursed the ground with thorns. Thorns are intruders.

2. Then in Exodus 3: 2 God appears to Moses from the midst of a thorny bush. The thorny bush was burning, but the bush was not consumed. This incident is referred to by both Jesus and Stephen in Luke 20: 37 and Acts 7: 30, respectively. Thorns are the consequence of sin. God promised deliverance and redemption from the midst of a *burning*

thorn bush. I find it thought-provoking that God, who cursed the ground with thorns, now reappears in the midst of thorns, promising deliverance!

3. Then God chose Acacia wood (Exodus 26: 26), from a small tree or bush whose branches are covered with long thorns, to build the tabernacle. The prepared thorn wood would be overlaid with gold (Exodus 26: 29). God took a cursed element of the fall and gave it beauty by His grace.

4. The place where Israel encamped last before entering the Promised Land was called Abel-Shittim, which means "Field of Thorns" (Numbers 25: 1; Joshua 2: 1). Isn't it fascinating that the children of Israel passed from the curse of thorns to the blessing of promise?

5. However, the role of thorns in the history of our redemption reaches its dramatic climax when Jesus is crucified wearing a crown of sharp and penetrating thorns. The "thorns and thistles" now become Jesus' crown as He conquers the curse of sin and death forever. Our sin that caused thorns to mar God's creation now pierced Christ's brow. He bore our thorns on the cross.

This sequence is worthy of a lengthy period of meditation. Thorns represent a grave problem from which we need redemption. They are aggressive and greedy competitors to the life of God in our hearts.

Let's Read:

> "And some seed fell among thorns; and the thorns grew up and choked it and it yielded no crop" (Mark 4: 7, NKJV).
>
> "Now these are the ones sown among thorns; they are the ones who hear the word, and the cares of this world, the deceitfulness of riches, and the desire for other things entering in choke the word, and it becomes unfruitful" (Mark 4: 18, NKJV).

We know from the text (Mark 4: 7, 18) that this heart was soft and had the right depth of soil to receive God's seed. It showed much promise as God's seed began to grow. However, it could not ripen because its life was choked by cohabiting and competitive thorns. We need to be aware that to leave thorns unchallenged in our hearts has devastating spiritual consequences. Jesus calls the deadly thorns: "The cares of this world, the deceitfulness of wealth and the desire for other things". All three vie with God's seed for first place in our hearts. If we value our relationship with Jesus above all other, we need to be astute and alert to what God says has the power and influence to ruin it. This third soil allows Satan to use thorns as a predator, and thorns win!

Thorns appear and grow as a result of spiritual laziness, foolishness and indifference. Natural thorns are known to insidiously feed their insatiable appetites. Spiritually, they aggressively and greedily compete with God's seed for the *same* light, air, space, water and nutrients. Over time, if thorns go unchecked and are not removed, they will grow extensively, overshadowing and overwhelming everything God has attentively planted and nurtured in our hearts. They are life sappers! Proverbs 24: 30–34 tells us that it was thorns and weeds that caused poverty and ruin.

The Most Dangerous of All

This kind of soil is the most dangerous of all and the one that has blinded and trapped many Christians today. Satan is successfully duping us into believing thorns carry no real danger. Whereas the heart with the second kind of soil was captive to sin, this heart is not necessarily doing anything it would consider sinful or harmful. This heart lives what it considers to be a healthy and balanced lifestyle – not too spiritual and not too worldly. It is proud of its ability to identify with nonbelievers, even emulating their ways to achieve a relationship. These believers enjoy all life offers: a good social life, materialism, an expansive entertainment and hi-tech market, beautiful sights, wonderful places to visit, and a meaningful church experience to finish off the week. Life may feel complete, but they are not only foolish in constantly placing themselves in danger of the sinful contamination of the world, but they lack wise judgment as to the power of thorns.

We are a generation enticed and lured by money, entertainment, and pleasure, and it is exactly these activities that compete with the seed of the kingdom of God in our hearts. Acting like thorns, Jesus says the "cares of this world, the deceitfulness of wealth and the desire for other things" (Mark 4: 18, NKJV, emphasis added) will slowly choke the life and vitality of the Word from our lives, rendering us spiritually powerless. The presence of thorns increasingly blunts our spiritual cutting edge, surrendering and relinquishing a "reverential fear of the Lord". This is what God says is the "fear of the Lord":

> "The fear of the LORD is the beginning of wisdom; a good understanding have all those who do His commandments. His praise endures forever" (Psalm 111: 10 NKJV).

> "In the fear of the LORD there is strong confidence, and His children will have a place of refuge. The fear of the LORD is a fountain of life, to turn one away from the snares of death" (Proverbs 14: 26–27 NKJV).

> "The fear of the LORD is to hate evil; pride and arrogance and the evil way and the perverse mouth I hate" (Proverbs 8: 13–14 NKJV).

No doubt God gave us many things for our enjoyment, but when they occupy, control, and sap the major part of our attention, time, and resources, relegating our relationship with God and the commands of His Word to the dregs of our life, there is something critically wrong. We are in spiritual danger.

The Divided Heart

A heart that nurtures both thorns and God's seed is a divided heart. This divided heart may happily attend church services, listen carefully to messages, have all the right spiritual terminology, raise its hands sincerely in worship, give an offering, pray, and exhibit all the outward signs of a vibrant Christian life. However, scratch the surface of priorities and you will find that it holds tight to "the best of both worlds". Those with divided hearts may not have any easily identifiable or evident sinful patterns in their lives, but their spiritually dull and sleepy hearts have little desire for the deeper things of God that require sacrifice and whole-hearted consecration. Their hearts are divided between the kingdom of God and worldly pleasure. It is a sinful division. A Sunday-morning service suffices as their "God-time" and they feel little or no compulsion or need for personal Bible study, sharing spiritual time with other believers, or spending devoted time in prayer. They will often tell you they want to, but they are just too busy with their job, home, hobbies, travel, etc. Spiritual growth may flourish for a while, but soon it wanes into mediocrity. They grow, but their growth is stunted; they may produce fruit, but it is nothing edible – just small, sour, bitter, and underdeveloped fruit, the fruit of thorns. You see, it is the "what else" that occupies our hearts that is deadly, choking spiritual growth. What a warning this is to those who think they can happily and successfully oscillate between two kingdoms: the kingdom of God and Satan's kingdom. Such thought completely underestimates the competitive superiority of thorns.

Let's be brutally honest. We are consumed with cares, riches, and the pleasures of life. We spend most of our money on ourselves, and we use our time in the pursuit of personal happiness. *We* are the selfish focus of our lives. We spend more time in front of the TV, or on getting fit, or going on holiday, or on the Internet, or watching movies, or reading magazines than we do in the presence of Jesus or in His Word. None of these activities may be regarded as "sinful", so we feel they are not harmful. But in reality, if you take what Jesus says seriously, these activities are already performing Satan's strategy of distraction, creating spiritual lethargy, insidiously choking our spiritual growth, and stunting possible development. The believer is being robbed of the kingdom of God.

Let Israel Be Our Object Lesson

The history of the children of Israel teaches us the same lesson. She (Israel) was constantly weakened and defeated in falling prey to the ways and pleasures of the surrounding and resident nations, compromising her relationship with God. Her heart was divided between what God had laid down as loving, protective, and godly boundaries and what she thought she could sneak in as innocuous extra thrills and entertainment. Israel was deceived and shipwrecked in her own thinking. Her disobedience and the resulting "thorns" choked out the life of God. She did not believe in the competitive superiority of thorns! Just as God warned Israel, we are warned in the parable of the sower:

> "But if you do not drive out the inhabitants of the land from before you, then it shall be that those whom you let remain shall be irritants in your eyes and thorns in your sides, and they shall harass you in the land where you dwell. Moreover it shall be that I will do to you as I thought to do to them" (Numbers 33: 55–56 NKJV).

Do you remember David's heart-wrenching cry after he played around with thorns? "Teach me your way, O LORD, and I will walk in your truth; give me *an undivided heart*, that I may fear your name" (Psalm 86: 11 NIV, emphasis added).

The thorny and divided heart will never know the beauty of union with Christ until it has completely dealt with the mixed and destructive forces that occupy it. Thorns overrun, take possession, choke the "opposition" and steal all the available resources. Spiritual growth may not be completely choked immediately—this is why we excuse thorns—but growth will be slowed down to the point that fruit never ripens. The spiritual parallel is evident. Thorns multiply profusely and we ignore that to our peril. Their seeds will also root and grow; therefore they must be uprooted entirely.

Killing a Thorn Tree

Wikipedia says, "Thorn trees can be killed using one of two approaches. *The first* and more historical approach is to use *slash and burn*. To start, the bark must be cut into around the bottom of the tree. The cut should go all the way around the tree and be at least two inches from bottom of cut to top. This is a slow process as you must ensure the bark is not able to heal and that the wound continues to stay open. After a year or two, the tree will begin to die and rot. It is better in most cases to burn the tree close to where it is felled so as not to scatter the thorns and promote growth elsewhere. Thorns can flatten tires even on the thickest tractor tires. The *second* approach is to *saw down the tree, leaving about a foot stump*. Douse the stump with a brush-killing spray. Crossbow [brand] spray works very well. Perhaps both approaches could be combined" (www.Wikipedia.com, emphasis added). Thorns are aggressive, not passive, making certain that a choice must be made for either thorns or the seed of God. The decision is ours!

Make up Your Mind

To be born-again is to change citizenship. Once we belonged to the kingdom of darkness, but now we belong to the kingdom of God. Once we walked in disobedience, but now we walk in obedience to God and His Word by the power of the Holy Spirit. Once we did what we liked when we liked, but now we are led by the Holy Spirit. We may once have spent our money how we liked, but now it is God who governs our finances. Everything we have is His!

> "No one can serve two masters; for either he will hate the one and love the other, or else he will be loyal to the one and despise the other. You cannot serve God and mammon [money, riches, and worldly goods])" (Matthew 6: 24 NKJV).

> "If anyone comes to me and does not hate his father and mother, wife and children, brothers and sisters, yes, and his own life also, he cannot be my disciple. And whoever does not bear his cross and come after me cannot be my disciple. For which of you, intending to build a tower, does not sit down first and count the cost, whether he has enough to finish it – lest, after he has laid the foundation, and is not able to finish, all who see it begin to mock him, saying, "This man began to build and was not able to finish". Or what king, going to make war against another king, does not sit down first and consider whether he is able with ten thousand to meet him who comes against him with twenty thousand? Or else, while the other is still a great way off, he sends a delegation and asks conditions of peace. So likewise, whoever of you does not forsake all that he has cannot be my disciple" (Luke 14: 26–33 NKJV).

God's call to be His disciple is both individually radical and mutually submissive within the body of Christ. His terms and conditions of discipleship include all of our heart, mind, and soul. In welcoming God's seed into our hearts, we haven't entered into some kind of informal and all-inclusive club where we can negotiate our special terms within a chummy arrangement. God is not our "mate". We have entered into a sober and committed bond, a new covenant with an Almighty and Sovereign God. It is God our Father who longs to deliver His people from the evil destruction of thorns, and He will faithfully do this by fire! It is the refiner's fire that purifies our heart (Matthew 7: 15–20; Malachi 3: 2; 1 Corinthians 3: 11–15). Review Part II introduction, "Evolving in the Presence of Fire".

The Cares of This World

Read Mark 4: 18

> "... they are the ones who hear the word and the cares of this world choke the word, and it becomes unfruitful".

The "cares of this world" are thorns and act like thorns. They overwhelm confidence and trust in God and will lead us into unbelief. Instead of meditating on God's ability to provide what we need and protect us from evil, we spend hours worrying about providing for and protecting ourselves. "Cares and worries" can be divided into three categories: provision, protection, and purpose. Because God has covenanted to provide all three we can confidently look up to our covenant partner and quit worrying!

The part of you that worries is the same part that meditates on God's ability and faithfulness, which is why you need to choose either one or the other. *Worry* chokes the life out of *faith!* As the days get darker and more difficult, so Satan will seek to overwhelm our hearts with the cares of this world.

> "And which of you by worrying can add one cubit to his stature? If you then are not able to do the least, why are you anxious for the rest? Consider the lilies, how they grow: they neither toil nor spin; and yet I say to you, even Solomon in all his glory was not arrayed like one of these. If then God so clothes the grass, which today is in the field and tomorrow is thrown into the oven, how much more will He clothe you, O you of little faith? And do not seek what you should eat or what you should drink, nor have an anxious mind. For all these things the nations of the world seek after, and your Father knows that you need these things. *But seek the kingdom of God* and all these things shall be added to you.

Do not fear, little flock, for it is your Father's good pleasure to give you the kingdom. Sell what you have and give alms; provide yourselves money bags which do not grow old, a treasure in the heavens that does not fail, where neither thief approaches nor moth destroys. For where your treasure is, there your heart will be also" (Luke 12: 25–34 NKJV, emphasis added).

The Consequences of Allowing the 'Cares of This World' to Rule Our Heart:

- Cares choke spiritual ambition and paralyse spiritual aspiration.
- Cares create fear, and fear creates worry; cares, fear, and worry choke faith. Truly knowing God frees us from the prison of worry. If we only realised *Who* now takes care of us, providing, protecting, comforting, and consoling us in all our ways, we would relax.
- Cares and worries tend to trap us in the present; they rob us of time and energy and potentially of our health.
- Cares and worries rob us of future hope. Their paralysing effect imprisons us in the pressures that engulf us, and very soon, despair and depression set in.
- Cares and worries also cause us to become so preoccupied and obsessed with what is in our mind that we are blind to what really needs our attention.

What Are Cares?

Some say life is about worry. Consider the following examples:

- Household bills, debt, and unemployment
- Students worry about school
- Graduates worry about getting jobs and paying off their loan debt
- Parents worry about their children's education and future

- Some people worry about their visa (immigration) status
- Others worry about buying cars and houses
- Older people worry about their health
- People worry about the effects of growing crime
- People worry about what someone else thinks or is saying
- Parents worry about their children's marriages
- Children worry about their aging parents
- Spouses worry about what the other will do if the spouse dies

Worry or Faith?

- *Faith* is defined as trusting in God's faithfulness. *Worry* comes from Satan, and simply put, it is not trusting in God's faithfulness, and that is the sin of unbelief.
- *Faith* means to rest completely in God's character, His ability and His faithfulness. *Worry* means to rely on self – we unsuccessfully try to carry the responsibility of solving life's problems. *Worry* centres on "me", having faith in "my" ability to provide.
- *Faith* combats *worry*! Knowing God, His character, nature, and ways is key to sustaining faith. Knowing God is becoming one with Him, like mixing two balls of clay until you cannot distinguish either; it's not just rational knowledge.
- *Faith* is not galvanised by oft repeating, "I must have more faith". We do not have the power to increase our faith. We need to understand that the focus should not be *our faith* but His faithfulness. To believe is to have faith in His faithfulness, His unchanging character. We do, however, have the responsibility towards God to:
    - Have a clean heart so the Word is free to root and grow.

  - Let the Word of God dwell in us richly and with all wisdom (Colossians 3: 16).

- *Faith* grows when the Word of God is active in our hearts (Romans 10: 17). *Worry* is magnified in the absence of the Word of God. For that very reason we need to have the Word of God profusely sown into our hearts. We can increase faith by reading the wonderful Bible stories that reveal God's character.
- *Faith* is not static, it is engaging and active. *Faith* means we are more than an admiring spectator. *Faith* always moves toward its object. Peter would never have grown in faith by staying in the boat; he believed and stepped out onto the water, trusting Jesus. We must step out in faith, and Jesus' faithfulness will step toward us!
- *Faith* is increased and multiplied as we specifically name and hand over each of our worries, choosing to trust God. It is faith-building to watch Him faithfully work out the answers to our needs.

Someone once said, "It is easy for fear or worry to replace faith because they have something in common: both challenge you to believe what you can't see is about to happen".

Remember what Jesus said: "Therefore I tell you, *do not worry about your life*, what you will eat or drink; or about your body, what you will wear. But seek first his kingdom and his righteousness, and all these things will be given to you as well" (Matthew 6: 25, 33, NKJV, emphasis added).

> "Rejoice in the Lord always. Again I will say, rejoice! Let your gentleness be known to all men. The Lord is at hand. *Be anxious for nothing*, but in everything by prayer and supplication, with thanksgiving, let your requests be made known to God; and the peace of God, which surpasses all understanding, will guard your hearts and minds through Christ Jesus" (Philippians 4: 4–7, NKJV, emphasis added).

Jesus doesn't ask us to pretend we have no worries; He knows life brings tremendous concerns. Jesus says active faith in God's faithfulness,

His righteousness, and His kingdom provides all the answers to our worries! Worry looks to self, faith looks to God.

A Selah Moment

Pause and think about that.

Prayer

"Lord, I do not want to be trapped in worry that chokes faith. I want to grow in faith and trust You to meet every need of my life. Help me. Lord, increase my faith as I let Your Word dwell in my heart richly and with all wisdom. Please lead me to passages of Scripture that reveal who You are; I want to know *You*. Please help me identify my preoccupations and help me take my eyes off myself and focus on You. Teach me more about Your covenant love. Amen".

Questions to Consider and Answer

We are largely unaware of what causes us to worry. Only when we sit down and consider how we spent our week will light dawn. To come to terms with "the cares of this life" do this short exercise:

- Make a list of what you did during the last seven days, day by day. Use your diary to jog your memory!
    - Under each activity, list the sorts of things you had to think about. Use single words.
    - Then list any worries associated with each activity.

Identifying our worries does not help, until we go a step further and bring them to Jesus. To first seek His kingdom means seeking first His rule, His reign, and His sovereignty. In other words, rather than worrying, you intentionally place your faith in His faithfulness. The worry-thorns are killed by repenting of unbelief and nurturing active faith in God's faithfulness.

- Using Matthew 6: 25, 33, fill in the blank spaces as prescribed and then read aloud the personalised version of the Scripture:

  "Therefore I tell you, ___________ [enter your name], do not worry about ___________, ___________, ___________ [enter the worries from your list]. But seek first His kingdom and His righteousness, and all these things will be given to you as well".

- Now turn every worry into a prayer: "Lord, I repent of unbelief that has trapped me in worry. Thank you, Lord, that Your faithfulness will meet _____________ and _________ and _________" (enter each worry).

Life Group

Each of us has some of the thorns Jesus describes in the parable of the sower.

  - Which "thorns" did you become aware of as you read Chapter 8?
  - How are those thorns affecting you?
  - Have you seen the "thorns" Jesus describes affect the life of someone you know? Please do not use names, just describe what you observed.

- Give feedback to the group about the exercise on worry.
  - Share what has been worrying you and how it has affected your faith. How have you been turning worry into faith in God's faithfulness?
- Finish your time together in prayer. Be specific when presenting your needs to the Lord.
- Before you leave, discuss the idea of taking up a "thanksgiving offering" next time you meet. The study is about sowing and reaping, which can include financial sowing and reaping. If you choose to

take up an offering, pray as a group about whom it should be given to as a blessing. Your offering may remove someone's worry!

Scripture for Meditation

"Beware of false prophets, who come to you in sheep's clothing, but inwardly they are ravenous wolves. You will know them by their fruits. Do men gather grapes from thorn bushes or figs from thistles? Even so, every good tree bears good fruit, but a bad tree bears bad fruit. A good tree cannot bear bad fruit, nor can a bad tree bear good fruit. Every tree that does not bear good fruit is cut down and thrown into the fire. Therefore by their fruits you will know them" (Matthew 7: 15–20 NKJV).

Chapter 9:

The Deadly Competition of Thorns

The Deceitfulness of Wealth

In this chapter, we continue to consider the deadly competition of thorns with God's seed. We have recognised that the 'cares of this world' root and rise up to stifle faith. We now consider the two other types of thorns that Jesus identified, 'the deceitfulness of wealth' and the 'desire for other things'. Peaceful coexistence between thorns and God's seed is not a biblical option. We are forced to decide, either we kill the thorns or God's seed in our hearts is choked of life.

Read Mark 4: 7

> "And some seed fell among thorns; and the thorns grew up and choked it, and it yielded no crop" (NKJV).

Read Mark 4: 18–19

> "Now these are the ones sown among thorns; they are the ones who

hear the word ... and the deceitfulness of riches and the desire for other things choke the word, and it becomes unfruitful" (NKJV).

The Bible reveals that God considers wealth an integral part of His covenant blessing, but He has far more in mind than just money in the bank. Wealth is the sum total of every benefit God has given us in life: good health, family, friends, personal privileges, peace, beautiful surroundings, as well as material blessings like property assets, jobs, cars etc. Wealth was, and is, a glorious expression of God's extravagant covenant love and provision. It is He who gave His people, Israel, the power and ability to acquire it (Deuteronomy 8: 18).

God blessed Abraham, Isaac, and Jacob, and their descendants still enjoy all the covenant benefits of His faithfulness. However, this was His warning to the children of Israel:

Read Deuteronomy 8: 11–14, 17–18

"Beware that you do not forget the LORD your God by not keeping His commandments, His judgments, and His statutes which I command you today, lest – when you have eaten and are full and have built beautiful houses and dwell in them; and when your herds and you flocks multiply, and your silver and gold are multiplied, and all that you have is multiplied; when you heart is lifted up, and you forget the LORD your God who brought you out of Egypt, from the house of your bondage ... *then you say in your heart, 'My power and the might of my hand have gained me this wealth'.* And you shall remember the LORD your God, for it is He who gives power to get wealth, that He may establish His covenant which He swore to your fathers, as it is this day" (NKJV, emphasis added).

Moses Warns Israel: Don't Be Deceived By Your Wealth

Moses warns the children of Israel of the danger of being deceived into thinking their wealth was accumulated due to their own abilities. It is God alone who gives the ability, endurance, and capacity to acquire wealth; to believe otherwise is a sin against God, our provider. What a danger presents itself, particularly for those in salaried employment today. Because we have a job with a good salary, we may be tempted to believe it was our own doing. And, we may be tempted to wrongly think that what is earned belongs to us and may be used as we wish. Wealth has seductive power to lure us into its control by making us believe that it is in our control. We need to make sure we have God's view on Who is the provider, and to Whom wealth belongs!

Jesus Warns Us

In the parable of the sower, Jesus speaks about the same truth when He equates the deceitfulness of wealth with thorns. Let's be absolutely clear. Jesus does not condemn wealth; how can He when it is His Father's blessing? However, He communicates the same stern warning Moses gave the children of Israel. If, in the acquisition of wealth, we act unrighteously or with pride claim it as our own, we are apt to fall prey to Satan's deception.

Jesus summed up the perils of wealth by declaring, "No man can serve two masters; for either he will hate the one and love the other, or else he will be loyal to the one and despise the other. You cannot serve God and mammon [wealth, power]" (Matthew 6: 24 NKJV).

It is typical of Satan to seek to corrupt such blessing, by seducing our hearts to centre on selfish ambition, superiority, greed, and stinginess. This leads people to manipulate, control, and prey on those who are in need. When one is rich and another poor, the situation could lead to a master-slave relationship. This may be seen in the relationship of the West with poor nations or between social classes. Do you realise withholding help when you have the ability to give and free someone of a burden is all part of Satan's wicked scheme? Sadly, Satan also has a grip on the wealth of many Christians, as is evident by the presence of thorns in their lives.

Let me emphasise that in keeping with the characteristics of thorns, the deceitfulness of wealth insidiously satisfies *its own* insatiable appetite. It competes ruthlessly with God's seed for the *same* light, air, space, and nutrients, and it consumes the moisture in the soil for its own purposes. This thorn does not rise up to attack God's seed; it simply slowly starves the life of God's seed in a born-again believer. It smothers and overwhelms God's seed. Jesus does not seek to eliminate wealth, He seeks to expose and destroy the *deceitfulness* of wealth. There is a difference! This deceit may operate in the lives of both the wealthy and the needy believer. Wealth is not evil, but the *deceitfulness* of wealth is. As we continue with this study, keep this key question in mind: *To whom does wealth belong*?

When Does Wealth Become Deceitful?

Consider the following summary:

- Wealth becomes deceitful when it controls and possesses us; it dictates, puffs up, and glorifies itself.
- Wealth becomes deceitful when we no longer recognise that we are blessed in order to bless others.
- Wealth becomes deceitful when we view it as a right, to be used as we wish. This can become a stumbling block, in particular to those who have a superior income, inherited wealth or hold a salaried job.

Wealth is given by God, and in the kingdom of God we are stewards under His instruction. Therefore, share acquired wealth, great or small, with joy and generosity. When we hold on to wealth so tightly that we no longer share what we have, joy in the Holy Spirit will diminish–it is choked.

The book of James makes it clear that deeds must accompany faith (James 2: 14-17). If we see a brother or sister in need, wishing him or her well won't help much. That is the time to be generous and meet his or her need! Ask the Holy Spirit to train you in being sensitive to others' needs. Pray for a "word of knowledge" (one of the lovely gifts of the Holy Spirit, 1 Corinthians 12: 8). Then the Holy Spirit can direct your giving to where He knows there is need. This is an exciting dimension of walking in the Spirit! Carry some extra money in your wallet or purse, with the sole purpose of being ready to give away as directed by the Holy Spirit.

- Wealth deceives you when what you have or don't have becomes the basis of obedience or disobedience.

As disciples of Jesus, our immediate response to God's call should be, "Yes, Lord!" Our obedience should not be based on whether or not we initially have the money. When wealth has a stranglehold on us, we are not able to free ourselves from the trappings of materialism for the sake of the Gospel.

- Wealth becomes deceitful when we have a greater passion for "me, myself, and I" – as in clothing or entertaining ourselves or adorning our homes – than for funding the work of the kingdom of God.

The motivation for accumulation of wealth is based on self-interest: we are keen to buy a bigger house, a smarter car, and designer clothes, have good holidays, or pay for a fitness club membership. But when it comes to giving toward evangelism, supporting a missionary, or sending aid to the poor, we find it hard to consider even the smallest amount per month.

- Wealth becomes deceitful when you attribute what you have to your own ability.

We elevate our importance and ability when we say in our hearts, "My power and the might of my hand have brought me this wealth". What a huge thorn of pride!

- Wealth has deceived when we believe wealth supplies all our needs. Wealth is not the supplier of our needs, God is. The deceitfulness of wealth competes with God for our trust and faith; it fuels selfish ambition. Satan whispers, "If wealth provides it all, why do you need God?"

Paul says to Timothy, "Now godliness with contentment is great gain. For we brought nothing into this world, and it is certain we can carry nothing out. And having food and clothing, with these we shall be content. But those who desire to be rich fall into temptation and a snare, and into many foolish and harmful lusts which drown men in destruction and perdition. For the love of money is a root of all kinds of evil, for which some have strayed from the faith in their greediness, and pierced themselves through with many sorrows" (1 Timothy 6: 6–10 NKJV).

- Wealth becomes deceitful when we buy beyond our means. It fuels discontent, loads unhealthy stress, and causes restlessness.

We are deceived into thinking that we can and must have anything we desire. Never is this more clearly seen than in the lust for the next technologically advanced computer, phone or gadget. The sin lies not so much in the purchase of the next level of computing, it lies in the fact that our giving to the needs of the body of Christ is so utterly stingy in comparison! We no longer exercise patience or godly restraint. Neither do we submit our requests to God for His approval and provision; a lust for things drives our buying, trapping us. Sometimes we may look for God's approval, but let's be very careful that we are not receiving guidance according to the idol of our hearts. (Ezekiel 14: 4–5) We readily spend large sums of money on the latest gizmo, but vehemently resist giving to the Lord and His kingdom. We are deceived when we say that we don't have enough to give!

The way to begin breaking this kind of satanic stronghold is to profane mammon. The next time we want something new and the old is working perfectly fine, let's give away the full amount of money we would have spent. It is likely to be a large amount of money, so resist all temptation and excuses to make the amount smaller. Give it away to the local church, a friend in need, a charity that eliminates suffering or a missionary. In doing so the stranglehold of Satan in our heart has begun to be broken. It is guaranteed that the very powerful spirit behind mammon will put up a huge fight not to give it away! That of itself may indicate that we are under the evil power of the deceitfulness of wealth.

Parents, consider carefully how many costly activities, in both time and money, your children need to be a part of. Peer pressure is fuelled by the spirit of the world. Choose a simple and modest lifestyle with your family.

It is a fierce spiritual battle to unlock our wealth in favour of the kingdom of God. We are certainly more deceived in this matter than most are aware.

Credit Card Debt

This is a good time to talk about credit card debt as the great deceiver of this age. This powerful, unruly and controlling thorn has all sorts of unhealthy and dangerous consequences; without doubt, it smothers and chokes spiritual life.

I have heard it said that the credit card interest payments of believers alone could fully fund every missionary endeavour around the world! At the very least our credit card *interest payments* rob God and His kingdom of vital resources. It is sad to realise that we may not have even considered giving the equivalent of the credit card interest payment to God's work, but we are content to let the bank have it! The lust for things is driven by the spirit of our age, and many of God's people have been enticed, deceived, and trapped by it.

Do we realise we lead our children right into the trap of the deceitfulness of wealth when we give in to everything they nag for? Giving in to have a peaceful life does not disciple a child in contentment and godliness. Do we understand that an evil power lurks behind advertisements to arouse sensuality and covetousness in our hearts? Until we face the fact that we have been seduced by the spirit of our age, we cannot fight it. We need to live *debt free* because debt interest alone robs God of significant amounts of money.

Malachi 3: 8–10 says, "Will a man rob God? Yet you have robbed Me! But you say, 'In what way have we robbed You?' In tithes and offerings. You are cursed with a curse, for you have robbed Me, even this whole nation. Bring all the tithes into the storehouse, that there may be food in My house, and try Me now in this," says the LORD of hosts, "if I will not open for you the windows of heaven and pour out for you such blessing that there will not be room enough to receive it" (NKJV).

Get Rid of Debt

Here are a few suggestions for getting rid of debt:

- In order to start living within your means, draw up a realistic and modest budget, eliminating all excesses and cutting back on nonessentials. Make a list of all your debt commitments, and draw up a careful plan to pay off your debt. If necessary, seek help. Your plan for paying off your debt forms part of your budget.

- Stick to your budget and stick to your plan. Make yourself accountable to a friend to do so. Our homes and lifestyles in the Western world bulge with vulgar excesses and nonessentials, while two-thirds of the world does not even have clean water, sanitation, and food. We can eat less, cook at home, exercise more, cut back on or eliminate alcohol, quit smoking, make do with the computers and mobile phones we have, and enjoy budget holidays. The excessive money spent for our comfort and enjoyment robs the kingdom of God. My own writing calls me to account! We are not only to live loving the Lord, but to live in the fear of the Lord.
- Never view the credit offered by the bank as extra purchase power or additional income. Impressive offers of credit deceive us into believing we can afford to become indebted to the bank. We forget that it comes at the cost of high interest rates and bondage to the bank! That is bondage to mammon.
- Should you have credit card debt, repent before the Lord—you have succumbed to the deceitfulness of wealth. Ask His help to break its stifling control in your life. Debt acts as a master in our lives, and we are its slave!
- Switch off advertisements on TV and destroy all unsolicited advertising flyers. Satan operates his evil work through the lust of the eyes. Refuse to be seduced.
- Train children to wait and save for the "must haves" of their generation.

- Decide to live a simple life. Enjoy recreational activities that are free. For instance, rediscover the joy of walking in the countryside, a picnic, a day on the beach or playing a team game in the local park.
- Starve gluttony before it starves our spiritual lives!

Many Missionaries Lead the Way

For the last twenty-three years it has been a privilege to serve missionaries who have sacrificed so much for the sake of the kingdom of God. Many missionaries live without a salary and know they have to depend on their heavenly Father for what they need. Travel to or from the mission field requires trusting the Lord for the money for an airfare; when filling their car with petrol, they are acutely aware God is supplying their fuel. When it comes to clothes, they talk to Father about their needs. Their position of having to completely rely upon God can seem vastly different to many believers back home. We can learn so much by listening to their stories of God's provision. Are they poor? Hardly. Spiritually, they are among some of the richest citizens of the kingdom of God you will ever meet; they demonstrate their love for Him in obedience and trust. They exhibit deep passion, joy, and contentment, and they are a living testimony. They are not trapped by the deception of wealth! I smile at people who want to flock around the rich and famous, even in Christian circles. They want to rub shoulders, drop their name, or be seen with them. Well, I want to exhort you to rub shoulders with "rich" and humble mission workers and let their faith rub off on you. Invite them for a meal, write a lovely thank-you card, and enclose a generous financial gift if you can. God will be so pleased with that act of giving!

Dependent or Independent?

Here is a stark contrast between the kingdom of darkness and the kingdom of God. The kingdom of God is all about dependence, depending on Him for all we need. The kingdom of darkness, under the control of Satan, is all about independence, looking to ourselves to provide our needs. The saying, "God helps those who help themselves" is not found in the Bible! Remember our key question: *To whom does wealth belong?* Well, the deceitfulness of wealth fools us into believing it belongs to us. True disciples of Jesus know wealth belongs to God, and are comfortable and content with it being under His lordship.

> "Command those who are rich in this present age not to be haughty, nor to trust in uncertain riches but in the living God, who gives us richly all things to enjoy. Let them do good, that they be rich in good works, ready to give, willing to share, storing up for themselves a good foundation for the time to come, that they may lay hold on eternal life" (1 Timothy 6: 17–19 NKJV).

Let's never forget, the *deceitfulness* of wealth actively produces life-robbing thorns. As those thorns are pampered, fed, overindulged and watered, they choke God's seed to where it never grows and flourishes. Let Jesus remind us, "Assuredly, I say to you that it is hard for a rich man to enter the kingdom of heaven. And again I say to you, it is easier for a camel to go through the eye of a needle than for a rich man to enter the kingdom of God" (Matthew 19: 24 NKJV).

How Much is Enough?

In our pursuit of a thorn-free heart, it is imperative to know what "enough" in terms of wealth is. Most of us have far more than we need. It is only when we establish what "enough" is that we know how much we have to give away – yes, give away, not save. Our "enough" budget should include modest savings, tithes and offerings.

> "Sell what you have and give alms; provide yourselves money bags which do not grow old, a treasure in the heavens that does not fail, where no thief approaches nor moth destroys. For where your treasure is, there your heart will be also" (Luke 12: 33–34 NKJV).

Don't you see the irony of the deceitfulness of wealth? We have houses filled with all the latest comforts, décor, gadgets, and technology while our spiritual lives lie barren and fruitless? Wealth preens the outward appearance, and dries up our spiritual lives. We should learn to be content with what we have (Luke 12: 16–21) and starve the life out of the thorns. Don't feed them!

Give Away!

God has blessed me with a beautiful home that I share with Mintie Nel, my co-worker and friend. We could only have dreamt of such an extravagant blessing from the Lord. After leaving Youth With A Mission in 1995, God led us to Worthing, on the south coast of England. God promised us, "Worthing will be a place of blessing". We possessed a campervan, a fridge freezer, a bookcase, and had a small amount of money in the bank. For some having so little would have been a concern, but for us it was a familiar missionary adventure with God. From relatively nothing, God chose to provide a home through the generosity of a Christian friend who believes in the special call of God on our lives. She gave from the wealth that God had given her. It was a humbling and extraordinary experience. Every time we enter our home we are conscious of God's incredible provision. We touch the walls and say, "Thank you, loving Father".

God calls us to generosity. Let's trawl our wardrobes, our houses, and our garages and determine what has not been used during the previous twelve months. Rather than selling, give possessions away. When we hear of a need let's always be willing to respond, no matter how small our gift. In the kingdom of God it isn't unusual to receive back the same amount we gave away—sometimes more—then we have money to give away again! The Lord may direct us to give ultra-sacrificially on some occasions. Perhaps we will hear the end of those stories in heaven. It is a wonderful way to live!

A few months back, Mintie bought a lovely new touch-screen mobile phone she hoped would help with the lack of dexterity in her crooked hands. She has severe rheumatoid arthritis in all her joints. I set it up for her, but within a few weeks it became apparent she was not using it. The touch screen was highly sensitive, and every time she touched one key, her awkwardly stiff fingers touched three others. Text messages were scrambled, and she was frustrated to the point of wanting to toss it out the window. The phone became an expensive ornament on the kitchen counter, and she finally resorted to using a cheap mobile phone with large keys, which she had acquired in South Africa.

A few weeks later a missionary couple from Haiti visited us for five days of debriefing. It came to light that the husband's mobile phone had died, leaving them stranded with no means of communication.

Mintie's face immediately lit up! "I have exactly the right telephone for you", she said with a chuckle.

She quickly disappeared into her small apartment, annexed to the main house, and returned with the lovely touch-screen phone and all its trimmings. "It's yours, with love from Jesus!" She could hardly contain her joy in giving it away; her body language shouted, "Hallelujah!"

You Cannot Out-give God

You simply cannot "out-give" God. As supported missionaries for more than thirty years, we are convinced that the reason why we have lacked nothing is because we have sown in accordance with the principles of the kingdom of God. We love giving; it gives us so much joy! We are wealthy in many ways, but we are intent not to allow wealth to control us. How about you?

> "And He said to them, 'Take heed and beware of covetousness, for one's life does not consist in the abundance of the things he possesses.' Then He spoke a parable to them, saying: 'The ground of a certain rich man yielded plentifully. And he thought within himself, saying, "What shall I do, since I have no room to store my crops?" So he said, "I will do this: I will pull down my barns and build greater, and there I will store all my crops and my goods. And I will say to my soul, 'Soul, you have many goods laid up for many years; take your ease; eat, drink, and be merry.'" But God said to him, "Fool! This night your soul will be required of you; then whose will those things be which you have provided? So is he who lays up treasure for himself, and is not rich towards God"'" (Luke 12: 15–21 NKJV).

Read 2 Corinthians 9: 6–11

How many uses of wealth can you identify?

1. ____.

2. ____.

3. ____.

Let's Examine Ourselves

Generosity helps loosen the grip of the deceitfulness of wealth. We all need to develop an attitude of giving generously – the giving of our time, of sharing our belongings, of sharing our homes and money, of helping practically, giving our expertise free of charge. Giving was the hallmark of true discipleship in the early Christian church.

Which of the following do you regularly practice? Mark those in *blue*. Which of the following are you prepared to practice? Mark those in *red*. You may want to add your own ideas to the list.

- Investing time and expertise in the life of another
- Intentional giving – listening to the Lord, preparing a gift, and delivering it
- Sharing your belongings
- Using a skill to help another, without payment
- Praying that others may excel
- Extending hospitality to fellow believers, including those on the perimeter of church fellowship
- Supporting an individual missionary on a monthly basis, thus involving your wealth in his or her well-being
- Sending cards of encouragement to those who serve you in the fellowship of the church
- Babysitting to allow a young couple some time together

- Helping an elderly or disabled person with his or her garden maintenance
- Taking an elderly person out in the car for a drive into the countryside
- Taking out friends for a meal
- Sending flowers to say you really appreciate and love someone
- Releasing someone from a debt to you
- Paying off someone else's debt
- Paying for a holiday for someone who has not been able to get away for some years
- Putting your caravan (camper) on a site for someone else to use and enjoy
- Opening your home for someone else to use while you are away on holiday (vacation)

A Selah Moment

Let's pause for a moment before we move on to the "desire for other things". In light of this chapter, ask yourself, "Am I being deceived by wealth?"

Prayer

"Lord, I am wealthy because You have blessed me, but have I become materialistic or covetous? Have I become unrestrained? Am I generous or am I miserly in my giving to the body of Christ? Have I become too comfortable in my home and with my belongings? Is there any need in another's life You would like me to meet? Please make me aware of specific thorns that are choking the life of Your seed in my heart and show me how to get rid of them. Bring me in humility and contrition to repentance. Amen".

The Desire for Other Things

Read Mark 4: 7

> "And some seed fell among thorns; and the thorns grew up and choked it, and it yielded no crop" (NKJV).

Read Mark 4: 18

> "Now these are the ones sown among thorns; they are the ones, who hear the word, and the deceitfulness of riches and the desire for other things choke the word, and it becomes unfruitful" (NKJV).

The Competition For Our First Love

By now you can be forgiven for wondering if there is much more to consider with regard to thorns. There is, however, one more aggressive and competing thorn Jesus wants to highlight: "The desire for other things". "Other things" compete for our first love.

Jesus wants to challenge the focus of our desires. On what are we spending our time, energy, and money? What occupies first place in our desires? Jesus is absolutely clear and direct when He says, "The desire for other things (that is things other than the things of the kingdom of God) will choke God's seed in your heart". What competes for our first love?

> "David cried to God, 'Teach me your way, O LORD, and I will walk in your truth; give me an undivided heart, that I may fear your name'" (Psalm 86: 11 NIV).

> "God said to Israel, 'I will give them an undivided heart and put a new spirit in them; I will remove from them their heart of stone and give them a heart of flesh'" (Ezekiel 11: 19 NIV).

What "other things" have captivated your heart? "Other things" are not necessarily sinful or wrong, but they are things that compete for your time, attention and love. We give many things a higher place and priority than the kingdom of God. So what are these "other things" we have set our hearts on? "Other things" can be distractions, preoccupations, or responsibilities, and they can be obsessions. They are the things we try to justify when they clash with the call to spend quality and extended time alone with Jesus and His Word! Let's consider: TV programmes, sports, fitness, recreation, hobbies, a particular friend, the latest technology, social media (e.g. Facebook and Twitter), iPads, iPods, Smartphones, iPhones, the internet, sexual gratification, video games, shopping, holidays, clubs, children, grandchildren, our body, health and physical appearance. How about church activities? You may add more to that list when you consider how you spend your time.

According to Galatians 5: 17, "other things" may also involve sins of the flesh that divert us from the things of the Spirit.

Read Galatians 5: 17–21

"For the flesh lusts against the Spirit and the Spirit against the flesh; and these are contrary to one another, so that you do not do the things that you wish. But if you are led by the Spirit, you are not under the law. Now the works of the flesh are evident, which are: adultery, fornication, uncleanness, lewdness, idolatry, sorcery, hatred, contentions, jealousies, outbursts of wrath, selfish ambitions, dissensions, heresies, envy, murders, drunkenness, revelries, and the like; of which I tell you beforehand, just as I also told you in time past, that those who practice such things will not inherit the kingdom of God" (NKJV). Galatians 6: 8 says sowing to the flesh makes it impossible to reap of the Spirit.

Other Things Can Become Idols

Any of the "other things" listed above can easily become idols. Idolatry means to allow someone or something other than Jesus to control our lives or be our life-source. Let's not deceive ourselves; we know when our heart is being gripped by someone or something else – we cannot get enough of him/her or it.

There is a serious warning in Judges 2: 1–4; God is jealous for our undivided love and loyalty. If we give our hearts away to "their gods", they will be *like thorns* constantly choking the life of God's seed in our hearts; our love for God will grow cold. Ungodly alliances rob God of the primary place in our hearts.

"Then the Angel of the LORD came up from Gilgal to Bochim, and said: "I led you up from Egypt and brought you to the land of which I swore to your fathers; and I said, 'I will never break my covenant with you. And you shall make no covenant with the inhabitants of this land; you shall tear down their altars.' But you have not obeyed my voice. Why have you done this? Therefore I also said, 'I will not drive them out before you; but *they shall be thorns in your side,* and *their gods* shall be a snare to you.'" So it was, when the angel of the LORD spoke these words to all the children of Israel that the people lifted up their voices and wept." (Judges 2: 1–4, NKJV, Emphasis added)

Summary

Remember, this thorny heart is certainly soft and has depth of soil. However, its softness and lack of spiritual wisdom makes it vulnerable to many seeds other than God's seed. It initially shows much promise as God's seed beds in, but it is the aggressive competitors that we have allowed to occupy our hearts that prevent God's seed from ever reaching its fruitful potential. The occupying thorns are the "cares of this world", "the deceitfulness of wealth", and the "desire for other things" (worldly pleasures).

If we choose to live with thorns their many seeds will multiply trouble; they will pierce us, tear our flesh, and draw blood. They will overwhelm and stifle spiritual aspiration, rendering our spiritual life unproductive. The only way to deal with thorns is to radically annihilate them. Let's shake off our apathy, show no mercy; dig them out from the root or burn them. This will require a radical assessment of what we worry about, how our wealth is affecting our attitude to God and the needs of His people, and whether our desires are wholly centred on pleasing God. If we are truly passionate about spiritual growth, we will make radical changes to remove the thorns. Let's remember Jesus' warning, "Enter by the narrow gate; for wide is the gate and broad is the way that leads to destruction, and there are many who go in by it. Because narrow is the gate and difficult is the way which leads to life, and there are few who find it" (Matthew 7: 13–14 NKJV).

This soil is the most dangerous of all because we are simply not aware, or we do not care that our contemporary twenty-first-century lifestyle is choking what should be a dedicated and undivided consecration to the Lord. Sadly, even after recognising this intense spiritual battle, many of us will remain lukewarm and indifferent—such is the stranglehold Satan has on our lives. The bottom line is: *To whom does our heart belong*?

Having a thorn-free heart is wonderful. When God's seed is able to take root and grow in uncluttered soil which is free of competition, we will find the life of the kingdom of God flourishing within us. That is the subject of our next chapter.

A Selah Moment

Let's stop and think about what has been said.

Prayer

"Lord, has wealth deceived me? Have worldly pleasures replaced intimacy with you? Are there thorns in my heart competing with the life of Your seed? Show me my heart. Help me reckon honestly with resident thorns and bring me to repentance and forgiveness. Lord, I want You to be my first love and for You to have the first place in my life. I desire that the field of my heart be filled with Your seed that is actively growing, shaping my life into the likeness of Jesus. Amen".

Questions to Consider and Answer

- What did you discover about yourself in this chapter?
    - What changes is God asking you to make?
    - Are you willing to meet His desire?
- Consider whether and how wealth, large or small, has deceived you. Make notes in your journal.
    - What changes are you going to make in your relationship to wealth?

Life Group

- Share what God has spoken to you about from this chapter.
- Discuss the changes you are going to make.
- Either share a story about how your own need was met through *the wealth and obedience of someone else,* or share a story about how *your wealth and obedience* met the need of someone else.
- Discuss how you *as a group* can be generous towards other people. If you have brought an offering, pray and agree on how to practically bless a particular person who needs help.

Scripture for Meditation

> "For the earth which drinks in the rain that often comes upon it, and bears herbs useful for those by whom it is cultivated receives blessing from God; but if it bears thorns and briers, it is rejected and near to being cursed whose end is to be burned" (Hebrews 6: 7–8 NKJV).
>
> "He who sows sparingly will also reap sparingly, and he who sows bountifully will also reap bountifully" (2 Corinthians 9: 6 NKJV).

Chapter 10:

The Good Soil

The parable of the sower describes four conditions of soil; all four types of soil heard the Word of God, but fruitfulness varied according to the condition of the soil.

- The *first soil* heard the Word of God, but the soil of the heart was hardened, and the Word could not penetrate. Satan preyed and easily stole the seed that had been sown. We can draw the conclusion that this person never experienced true regeneration of the spirit; because God's seed never entered the soil of his or her heart to bring new life.
- The *second soil* heard the Word of God and quickly accepted it, but the soil among the rocks was shallow, and the Word could only produce weak roots. Old patterns of sin in the form of rocks prevented roots going down deep, and the puny plants withered in the hot sun. This may represent a new believer in the kingdom, still struggling with his or her old life. It could also represent a lazy apathetic believer sitting in a pew week after week; ever hearing yet remaining unchanged.

- The *third soil* heard the Word of God and grew well because the soil was soft and had some depth, but care of the heart was neglected, and it became densely populated with thorns. Instead of removing the thorns, they were tolerated, seeded and grew rampantly, robbing God's seed of light, moisture and nutrients. The cares, the deceitfulness of wealth, as well as the pleasures of life, choked God's seed. This could represent a believer of any age who never considered that the cost of discipleship includes leaving the old life of the world, denial of self, taking up his or her cross, and following Jesus wholeheartedly.
- It is only the *fourth soil* that bore much fruit in measures of thirtyfold, sixtyfold, and a hundredfold. It is the good soil we now consider.

Read Mark 4: 8

> "But other seed fell on good (well-adapted) ground and yielded a crop that sprang up increased and produced some thirtyfold, some sixty, and some a hundred" (NKJV).

Read Mark 4: 20

> "But these are the ones sown on good (well-adapted) ground, those who hear the word, accept it, and bear fruit: some thirtyfold, some sixty and some a hundred" (NKJV).

Good Soil Has Had Obstacles Removed

Jesus tells us that the "good" soil ("well-adapted" soil, Amplified Bible) has three qualitative characteristics: it *hears* the Word of God, *accepts* the Word of God, and *bears fruit* as a result of the Word of God. The Word of God not only has entrance but it is welcomed and nurtured to fruitfulness by the presence of rich minerals and living water. Good soil is fertile soil, prepared and primed by the Holy Spirit.

This believer has squarely faced any sign of hardness, rocks, and thorns in their heart with a humble and meek attitude. He / she did not expect God to overlook hardness, resident rocks and thorns, he / she yielded to the plough. God's sanctifying work has made the soil ready to receive abundant seed. How different this is to the attitude that says, "I accept Jesus, but He must take me as I am"—meaning, "I am not changing, He must fit in with me and the lifestyle I choose!" Good soil is the result of God's regular ploughing. The presence of rich minerals like mercy, humility, kindness, and meekness make it easy for God's Word to bed in deeply, germinate and come to fullness and fruitfulness. The difference between this soil and the other three is that it has welcomed God's inspection of the heart and allowed Him to clear and clean it up.

James says, "Wherefore putting away all filthiness and overflowing of wickedness, receive with meekness the implanted word, which is able to save your souls. But be ye doers of the word, and not hearers only, deluding your own selves" (James 1: 21–22 NKJV).

Paul says, "Therefore, as the elect of God, holy and beloved, put on tender mercies, kindness, humility, meekness, longsuffering; bearing with one another, and forgiving one another, if anyone has a complaint against another; even as Christ forgave you, so you also must do" (Colossians 3: 12–13 NKJV).

Quality Soil Produces a Quality Disciple

When the quality of the soil is this good it provides an open channel to the voice of the Lord. His words are eagerly anticipated, treasured and never wasted; they are considered the life-blood of a disciple's life. How God must love this sort of eagerness and readiness to hear and receive from Him. He can easily share the secrets of His kingdom with a heart so ready, open, keen and alert.

Good soil is able to bear fruit in different measures: thirtyfold, sixtyfold, and even one hundredfold. The "thirtyfold" is designed to express the lowest degree of fruitfulness; the "hundredfold" the highest; and the "sixtyfold" the intermediate degrees of fruitfulness. The sense is that there is always greater fruitfulness to be obtained as we grow spiritually. The profusion of spiritual fruit makes this believer stand out in the crowd. They live above the level of spiritual mediocrity, like an eagle soaring on the thermals.

The Greek word translated as "good", is *kalos* and means that this soil is befitting, virtuous, honest, meek, well and worthy. To use a modern expression, this soil is "fit for its purpose" – God's purpose. This person with good soil in their heart walks worthy of the Lord (Colossians 1: 10).

We may be tempted to consider good soil as unique or exceptional. Some might consider it "above them". But, this is not God's view! In time, good and rich soil should be the experience of every disciple of Jesus. It should be our aim, and, it should be our aspiration and goal to help others produce good and rich soil. If you are now saying, "I cannot be like that!" you may be comforted to know you are right. *You cannot,* but *God can* create good soil in your heart by the power of the Holy Spirit. The question you need to answer before God is, "Are you willing to be changed to produce good soil?" Quality soil produces a quality disciple!

Fruitfulness for Whose Benefit?

But for whose benefit is fruitfulness? John 15: 8 reminds us that it is for the glory of our heavenly Father. "By this my Father is glorified, that you bear much fruit; so you will be my disciples". Fruitfulness displays His glory and is the hallmark of discipleship. A disciple of Jesus produces fruit that can be seen!

Fruitfulness is also for the benefit of others. It doesn't matter whether you are a church minister or a lay-person, rich or poor, young or old—God purposefully sows His Word *in us* in order to reproduce and multiply His life *through us*. We are called to be His grain store, filled with seed ready to be sown for the benefit of others. Each time we are generous, kind, understanding, forgiving, merciful, compassionate, and longsuffering towards others, it is His reproductive seed bearing fruit and being sown. Every time we testify to the truth of God's Word, teach or preach, we sow from our stored harvest of seed. All of us should be faithful in this task. The kingdom of God offers no "opt out" programme from God's reproduction process. We might not have been told, but when we were born-again of God's seed we signed up for reproduction!

> "You therefore, my son, be strong in the grace that is in Christ Jesus. And the things that you have heard from me among many witnesses, commit these to faithful men who will be able to teach others also" (2 Timothy 2: 1–2 NKJV).

Every believer is called to *"abide in Him and He in you, and bear fruit"* (John 15: 4, NKJV, emphasis added). We all need to meditate and act on this Scripture! Fruit is borne in good and well-adapted soil. A believer who is truly saved will reveal his or her salvation experience by the harvest produced. Fruit never lies.

The apostle John records the words of Jesus:

> "I am the true vine, and my Father is the vinedresser. Every branch in me that does not bear fruit He takes away; and every branch that bears fruit He prunes, that it may bear more fruit. You are already clean because of the word which I have spoken to you. Abide in me, and I in you. As the branch cannot bear fruit of itself, unless it abides in the vine, neither can you, unless you abide in me. I am the vine, you are the branches. He who abides in me, and I in him, bears much fruit; for without me you can do nothing. If anyone does not abide in me, he is cast out as a branch and is withered; and they gather them and throw them into the fire, and they are burned. If you abide in me, and my words abide in you, you will ask what you desire, and it shall be done for you. By this my Father is glorified, that you bear much fruit; so you will be my disciples" (John 15: 1–8 NKJV).

Wholehearted

One word that describes the good soil is "wholehearted". In the Bible there is no better example of "wholeheartedness" than King David who actively and consistently directed his heart towards God in worship and devotion. His whole life was oriented toward God, seeking His counsel and direction. Listen to David's heart speak in these Psalms:

"I will praise You, O LORD, with my whole heart; I will tell of all Your marvellous works. I will be glad and rejoice in You; I will sing praise to Your name, O Most High" (Psalm 9: 1–2 NKJV).

"I will bless the LORD who has given me counsel; my heart also instructs me in the night seasons. I have set the LORD always before me; because He is at my right hand I shall not be moved" (Psalm 16: 7–8 NKJV).

"When You said, 'Seek My face', my heart said to You, 'Your face, LORD, I will seek'" (Psalm 27: 8 NKJV).

David's wholeheartedness for God was never more poignantly seen than in his recognition of, and response to, failure. Interestingly, David failed but his undivided heart for God was immediately seen in the depth of his repentance. He ran to God for mercy!

King David honestly cried, "There is no soundness in my flesh because of Your anger, nor any health in my bones because of my sin. For my iniquities have gone over my head; like a heavy burden they are too heavy for me. My wounds are foul and festering because of my foolishness. I am troubled, I am bowed down greatly; I go mourning all the day long. For my loins are full of inflammation, and there is no soundness in my flesh. I am feeble and severely broken; I groan because of the turmoil of my heart. Lord, all my desire is before You; and my sighing is not hidden from You. My heart pants, my strength fails me; as for the light of my eyes, it also has gone from me" (Psalm 38: 3–10 NKJV).

Failure is inevitable for every disciple of Jesus and it may be accurately assessed as the greatest and most severe test to be faced. This is especially true for a leader in the body of Christ. Clearly, it is how we respond to failure that is critical not only for us personally but for those who emulate and follow us. Do we surrender to the Lord and admit our weakness and failings (that is the sign of good soil), or do we pretend with pride and arrogance that nothing has happened, ignoring our sinfulness (that is a sign of hardness, rocks or thorns)?

Paul reminds us of the reality of our earthiness in 2 Corinthians 4: 7–12 "But we have this treasure in earthen vessels, that the excellence of the power may be of God and not of us. We are hard-pressed on every side, yet not crushed; we are perplexed, but not in despair; persecuted, but not forsaken; struck down, but not destroyed — always carrying about in the body the dying of the Lord Jesus, that the life of Jesus also may be manifested in our body. For we who live are always delivered to death for Jesus' sake, that the life of Jesus also may be manifested in our mortal flesh. So then death is working in us, but life in you" (NKJV).

Good soil keeps a short account of sin with God and man. In failure it does not allow time to lapse where Satan can contaminate or rebuild any sort of stronghold in resistance to God.

A Summary of the Characteristics of Good Soil

- Good soil is *guarded.* It is careful with what it allows in through the eyes and mind, and to what it refuses access, e.g. gossip, lies, pornographic images, divisive talk, occult influence, heretical doctrine. The good soil fills itself with goodness and is vigilant against entrapment and contamination. It remains alert to temptation and influence from without.

"Finally, brethren, whatever things are true, whatever things are noble, whatever things are just, whatever things are pure, whatever things are lovely, whatever things are of good report, if there is any virtue and if there is anything praiseworthy – meditate on these things. The things which you learned and received and heard and saw in me, these do, and the God of peace will be with you" (Philippians 4: 8–9 NKJV).

- Good soil is *soft, humble, and contrite.* It knows the joy of freely forgiving and being forgiven. It is aware of its weakness, and in failure it is not only deeply penitent before God but is humble in its confession of wrongdoing to those it has sinned against. It is willing, even desirous, to be searched and cleansed. This heart does not want anything to spoil its relationship with God.
- Good soil is *upright and full of integrity.* This good soil loves

righteousness. God's Word is its plumbline. It bathes in truth, memorising, meditating, and musing on the ways of God. The soil is rich and fertile. It is to this soil that others turn for nurture, direction and encouragement—they know where to find life!

- Good soil is *holy soil*. It is honoured and respected as the *dwelling place of God*. Paul says, "Do you not know that you are the temple of God and that the Spirit of God dwells in you? If anyone defiles the temple of God, God will destroy him. For the temple of God is holy, which temple you are" (1 Corinthians 3: 16–17 NKJV).
- Good soil represents a *God-dependant and teachable heart*. It seeks the counsel of God's voice, consulting Him about everything. It is a heart that, having carefully counted the cost, chooses to forsake everything for His sake.
- Good soil is *loyal, devoted, and true*; a heart the Lord searches out.

  "For the eyes of the LORD run to and fro throughout the whole earth, to show Himself strong on behalf of those whose heart is loyal to Him" (2 Chronicles16: 8–9 NKJV). God said, 'Oh, that they had such a heart in them that they would fear me and always keep all my commandments, that it might be well with them and with their children forever!" (Deuteronomy 5: 29 NKJV).

  'Hear, O Israel: The LORD our God, the LORD is one! You shall love the LORD your God with all your heart, with all your soul, and with all your strength. And these words which I command you today shall be in your heart. You shall teach them diligently to your children, and shall talk of them when you sit in your house, when you walk by the way, when you lie down, and when you rise up" (Deuteronomy 6: 4–7 NKJV).
- *Good soil hears productively***.** It absorbs and retains the goodness of the Word of God. It knows that its purpose is to receive God's seed and bear fruit. This soil hears with eagerness and says, "Yes, Lord! Where, when, how? Send me."

Enrich the Good Soil

How can we enrich the good soil? Good soil needs to be maintained. The Bible teaches that *fellowship in the Spirit* enriches the soil of our hearts. This is how Acts 2: 42 describes that special fellowship:

> "And they continued steadfastly in the apostles' doctrine and fellowship, in the breaking of bread, and in prayers. Then fear came upon every soul, and many wonders and signs were done through the apostles. Now all who believed were together, and had all things in common, and sold their possessions and goods, and divided them among all, as anyone had need. So continuing daily with one accord in the temple, and breaking bread from house to house, they ate their food with gladness and simplicity of heart, praising God and having favour with all the people. And the Lord added to the church daily those who were being saved" (NKJV).

We need one another and the soil of our heart thrives on a shared and mutual lifestyle of love, spiritual encouragement, care and generosity. We are enriched and spurred on by sharing belongings and life. It is special to break bread, praying together in our homes. We are one body in Christ, and as such, members who belong to one another (Romans 12: 5). We cannot fail to be blessed when there is a strong and committed "one another" spirit present among those with whom we fellowship. There is no greater joy than being interdependent!

The opposite of interdependence is independence. We must be aware of Satan's strategy to pick off isolated and lone Christians in the same manner a roaring lion picks off its weak and vulnerable prey. (1 Peter 5: 8) First the lion separates its target and then it attacks to kill.

> "Let *us* draw near with a true heart in full assurance of faith, having our hearts sprinkled from an evil conscience and our bodies washed with pure water. Let *us* hold fast the confession of our hope without wavering, for He who promised is faithful. And let *us consider one another* in order to stir up love and good works, not forsaking the assembling of ourselves together, as is the manner of some, but exhorting one another, and so much the more as you see the day approaching" (Hebrews 10: 22–25, NKJV, emphasis added).

Good Soil Pays Dividends

We can still be bearing fruit in old age if we give careful attention to the soil of our heart. The psalmist says, "The righteous shall flourish like a palm tree; he shall grow like a cedar in Lebanon. Those who are planted in the house of the LORD shall flourish in the courts of our God. They shall still bear fruit in old age; they shall be fresh and flourishing, to declare that the LORD is upright; He is my rock, and there is no unrighteousness in Him" (Psalm 92: 12–15 NKJV).

A Selah Moment

Let's stop and think about what we have read.

Prayer

Let's use this beautiful Scripture once again as our prayer: "Create in me a clean heart, O God, and renew a steadfast spirit within me. Do not cast me away from Your presence, and do not take Your Holy Spirit from me. Restore to me the joy of Your salvation, and uphold me by Your generous Spirit" (Psalm 51: 10–12 NKJV).

Questions to Consider and Answer

- What are you doing to ensure your heart is full of good soil?
- How are you growing in intimacy with God?

Life Group

It may seem easier and more humble to talk about the things that are sinful or lacking in our hearts. However, in this life group, let's spend time sharing about the measure of good soil in our hearts.

- What attributes of good soil do you see in your life?
- What attributes of good soil do you identify in the lives of one another? Please share truthfully what you have come to see during the past weeks together.
- Describe how you give attentive care to the good soil in your heart.

Scripture for Meditation

> "Listen carefully to me, and eat what is good. And let your soul delight itself in abundance. Incline your ear, and come to me. Hear, and your soul shall live" (Isaiah 55: 2b–3 NKJV).

Chapter 11:

Life Group

Wrapping Up

This week we draw our discipleship season to a close; it is time to reflect and round off well. I suggest you read and consider this chapter in your life group. Appoint someone to read.

Do you remember the seed you were given at the beginning of this study? What happened to it? Has it been fruitful? Have you brought the plant, or a photo, with you?

Share

- Share what you did with the seed. What you did or did not do with it may be deeply significant. That in itself is a modern-day parable!
    - Did you plant it carefully or did you lose it?
    - What did it become?
    - Did you neglect it?

- How do you know it is healthy and alive?

Think and Discuss

Jesus teaches about the authority and power of God's seed. He desires to change and transform our hearts, but it is also clear that we have a significant part to play in allowing Him to clear the ground, prepare the soil, and plant the seed of His Word. We must allow the Holy Spirit to do His work of grace and healing. We are to *let* the word of Christ dwell richly in us—but how will we do that?

- Take a few minutes to think about the following Scripture and in particular the word "let". Think how you can "let" the word of Christ dwell richly in you.

  "*Let* the word of Christ dwell in you richly in all wisdom, teaching and admonishing one another in psalms and hymns and spiritual songs, singing with grace in your hearts to the Lord" (Colossians 1: 16, NKJV, emphasis added).

- Discuss in your group how, during this discipleship season, you have "let" God's Word not only *come into your heart* but also "let" it *work* in your heart. What have you experienced? What has been the fruit?

Read On

God's seed reproduces the nature of Jesus *in us*; we are to be *like Him*. In the parable of the sower, Jesus would have been referring to a small rough patch of Middle Eastern ground, possibly in the Galilee that displayed hard soil, rocks, thorns, and good soil. It was not a modern farm with modern farming methods! When he reflected on the soil He reflected on the heart of man.

Think and Discuss

In doing this study together we have reflected on the hardness, rocks, thorns and good soil of our hearts. We shared openly together. Answer the following questions:

- How did you feel when others started to open up their hearts?
- What impact did it have on your own life?
- What is the most life-changing revelation you received during the course of this study?

Read On

Jesus' explanation of spiritual growth is based on the natural laws of farming—sowing and reaping. From the beginning of creation, God programmed seeds to reproduce and multiply in order to fill the earth. It was ordained that growth is the evidence of life. Two things become clear in the parable of the sower:

1. There is no cheating in farming; fruitfulness is wholly dependent on what is planted. There is absolute integrity between what is sown and what is produced. You cannot circumvent a God-ordained natural law, because fruit never lies. Seed in means a crop out. No seed in is barrenness.
2. A healthy and abundant harvest is produced in protected, well-prepared, and nurtured soil.

Question for Each to Answer

- Reflecting on what we have learnt from the parable of the sower how does this change the way you will lead your life from now on?
    - How will you reprioritise to God's order of spiritual growth?
    - What will you do with God's seed?
    - How will you fill your heart and how will you guard your heart?
    - With what and with whom will you choose to spend time and share life?

Final Encouragement

Remember, when seeds are planted and while roots are developing, there is always much more going on beneath the soil than can be seen above the surface. Spiritual growth is not only about what we immediately see. Let's have faith in God's faithfulness for what we cannot see yet, both in ourselves and others. Be assured that what God sows deep into the soil of our hearts will burst through the soil with dynamic power in its proper season.

God will *prepare the soil* of our hearts but we must be willing to yield to the plough. A prepared and pure heart readily inclines itself toward the Sower with great expectation. God sows the Word into our hearts. Then, He watches over His Word to bring it to fruitfulness and multiplication. That is how the growth cycle of seed works. You won't always get immediate results, but God has sown the potential of a glorious harvest. Especially, let's remember this with new believers—growth takes time. We can rest and abide in Him with eager anticipation for what will be. Read John 15: 1–8.

Right in the beginning God said to Adam, 'Be fruitful and multiply, fill the earth and subdue it'" (Genesis 1: 28). May the Lord make us abundantly fruitful for His kingdom's sake.

Pray for Each Other

- Give thanks to the Lord for those with whom you shared this period of growing together.
- Thank the Lord for what you learned.
- Wait on the Lord for a special Scripture for each one and then turn that Scripture into a prayer of blessing.

Word Declaration

Finish by declaring Isaiah 55: 8–13 together:

> "'For My thoughts are not your thoughts, nor are your ways My ways', says the LORD. 'For as the heavens are higher than the

earth, so are my ways higher than your ways and my thoughts than your thoughts. For as the rain comes down, and the snow from heaven, and do not return there, but water the earth, and make it bring forth and bud, that it may give seed to the sower and bread to the eater, so shall My word be that goes forth from my mouth; It shall not return to me void, but it shall accomplish what I please, and it shall prosper in the thing for which I sent it. For you shall go out with joy, and be led out with peace; the mountains and the hills shall break forth into singing before you, and all the trees of the field shall clap their hands. Instead of the thorn shall come up the cypress tree, and instead of the brier shall come up the myrtle tree; and it shall be to the LORD for a name, for an everlasting sign that shall not be cut off'" (NKJV).

Another discipleship season

This book exhorts believers to allow God to clean up their hearts to receive the seed of His Word. But *how* does God's Word get firmly planted? How does the Holy Spirit engraft the Word of God into our hearts? The Bible exhorts us to "eat" the Word of God, but how do we do that? How do we ingest and digest the Word of God to the point where our souls are fed, transformed and satisfied? How can we hear the voice of the Lord and walk in obedience to His ways? What are the benefits of biblical meditation?

These questions will be considered in "Eat the Word"—the second book in our discipleship series. It is an exciting and life-changing lesson on biblical meditation for you and your friends to study together. It will be published through WestBow Press, a division of Thomas Nelson, shortly. We hope you will join us for another season of discipleship! In the meantime:

"The LORD bless you and keep you; the LORD make His face shine upon you and be gracious to you; the LORD lift up His countenance upon you, and give you peace" (Numbers 6: 24–26 NKJV).

Appendix

"The Gift of Forgiveness"

by Reuven and Yanit Ross

("The Gift of Forgiveness" is an excerpt from
The Lifestyle of a Disciple, Lesson #24.)

And forgive us our debts, as we forgive our debtors. For if you forgive men their trespasses, your heavenly Father will also forgive you. But if you do not forgive men their trespasses, neither will your Father forgive your trespasses. – Matthew 6: 12, 14–15

Forgiveness is always twofold: we receive God's love and forgiveness by faith, and we give love and forgiveness to others by faith. God expects us to forgive with the same abundance of mercy that He offers us. He does not want us to give small measures of mercy to others, but to heap it up on them extravagantly– just as He pours His mercy and forgiveness out on us without limit.

Jesus' Blood is Sufficient For All Sin

Read 1 John 1: 9 and Romans 8: 1. When we confess our sins to God and repent of them, He forgives us and cleanses us from all wrong. He does not condemn us. There may still be natural consequences of our sin, but the forgiveness is complete. The Devil condemns us by reminding us of our past failures; he loves to rob us of our peace and joy. However, the blood of Jesus is sufficient for all of our sin – past, present, and future. We can lawfully resist condemnation as soon as we confess our sin, repent towards God, and receive His forgiveness.

Forgiveness Leads to Healing

Forgiveness is an important key to freedom, victory, and joy. In fact, forgiveness is the key to all inner healing and transformation. Once we forgive, we can be healed of emotional pain and receive deliverance from demonic strongholds and oppression. We cannot attain wholeness without forgiving those who have wronged us.

Until we forgive, we are bound to the past and unable to live fully in the present. The bitterness we carry from our past painful relationships will affect our present relationships, defiling and damaging them. When we retain resentment by focusing on the wrong done to us, we *bind ourselves* to the one who inflicted the pain. The resulting bondage limits God's work in our lives and in theirs. It is as if we tie God's hands. As soon as we forgive, however, God is able to work in everyone involved.

When we judge another for his or her sin, we run the risk of developing that same hated sin in ourselves. According to Romans 2: 1, that which we are quick to see in others is already in us or is potentially in us.

Retaining Unforgiveness is Hazardous

Unforgiveness, according to Matthew 18: 34–35, can open the door to the enemy in our lives. The tormentors who are assigned to the unforgiving include depression, fear, doubt, strife, and disease. When we refuse to forgive, we open ourselves up to oppression, demonic harassment, and particular physical ailments. Unforgiveness eats away one's emotional and physical health.

If left unchecked, unforgiveness will progress towards deception and perversion. The process is gradual, beginning with real or perceived hurt. If the hurt is not cleansed and healed through forgiveness, that unforgiveness will lead to anger, which grows into resentment.

Matured resentment is bitterness. Bitterness leads to blame which develops into hatred. Rebellion follows hatred, making one susceptible to deception and self-deception. Once a person is deceived, he moves into moral sins easily, such as sexual perversion.

The destruction of unforgiveness follows this pattern: unforgiveness to anger, to resentment, to bitterness, to blame (condemnation), to hatred, to rebellion, to deception, to perversion, and other moral sins.

Bitterness is the seedbed for any demonic work! It is the result of unresolved revenge. The works of the flesh found in Galatians 5: 19–21 can always be traced back to bitterness, and even further back to an area of deep hurt or rejection.

Bitterness Must Be Rooted Out

Unforgiveness can sometimes be hidden, but once it has matured into a *root of bitterness*, it manifests itself through our speech, actions, reactions and attitudes. It defiles those with whom we interact. When a person has a root of bitterness, he or she tends to carry grudges and take on others' hurts easily. He will speak harshly or critically, overreact to minor injustices, and be ultra sensitive to rejection.

Read Hebrews 12: 15. The root of bitterness remains after the branches of resentment are cut off, allowing resentment to grow again easily when watered with more hurt. The bitterness must be rooted out, or else when offence reoccurs, unforgiveness and bitterness will follow.

Forgiveness is a Choice

Forgiveness is not a feeling; it is a choice of our will. We receive forgiveness by faith, and we extend it by faith, acting on our will to let the past go. We choose to forgive with Jesus' help and strength. We may not feel like forgiving at the point of our decision to forgive, but the positive feelings will come later as we continue praying for our offender.

Worldly psychology often encourages us not to forgive (so as not to show weakness), and then attempts to tell us how to cope with our pain and anger. Jesus, however, gives us the grace to release the debt and to overcome! The word "cope" is not part of Jesus' vocabulary, but the word "overcome" is!

We must die to ourselves – our resentment and desire for revenge – in order to overcome. We have to allow Jesus to mercifully forgive others through us. If we wait until we feel like forgiving in order to do so, we never will because our old fleshly nature loves to hold onto hurt and anger. Part of dying to self is learning to walk in forgiveness.

Read Colossians 2: 13–14. Forgiveness is handling others' debts as God handles ours – He cancels them. We are to forgive even if we never receive an apology, explanation, or some form of restitution. We release the offence, choosing never to look at it again. We "put it behind us" the same way God puts our sins behind His back (Isaiah 38: 17).

Confront When Necessary

There are times when forgiving from our hearts without confronting the offender will not sufficiently restore the relationship. The general rule is this: we should forgive in our hearts and cover the sin in love as much as possible. If the offence still bothers us and robs us of peace two or three days later, we should talk about it with the offender alone, as Matthew 18: 15 instructs.

When we repress and overlook offences without confronting those who caused the offence, we tend to withdraw our fellowship from them. Then, rather than growing in real relationship, we relate superficially and with distrust. To really be *one* in Christ, we need to have trusting relationships that involve transparency and forgiveness. We must *care enough* to confront the other person, talk out the hurtful situation, and be reconciled. Forgiveness should result in a restored, growing relationship. It is always *our* responsibility to seek peace, no matter who is at fault. Whether we are the wounded one or the guilty one, we are to seek peace and restoration (see Hebrews 12: 14).

Sometimes we *have* forgiven, but we still carry inner pain for a while. Our emotions may need some time and ministry from the Word to fully heal. Psalm 107: 20 says, "He sent His Word and healed them and delivered them from their destructions". Keep soaking in God's Word and His love, and in time the healing will come. Once you can pray for your offender with love and an open heart towards him or her, then you know your emotions have caught up with your choice of forgiveness. The sin that will hinder spiritual growth faster than anything else is unforgiveness! Do not allow yourself the luxury of retaining hurt and bitterness. It is not worth it.

A Pattern for Forgiving Others

First – Ask the Holy Spirit to reveal your own transgressions to you and then deal properly with them. You might want to list your sins and then repent, asking God for forgiveness (e.g., "I acknowledge my sin of_____ ______ to You, and ask You to forgive me", or "I am sorry I did _______ to ___________ and I ask for Your forgiveness"). Realize you must make restitution when necessary with the offended.

Second – Release the unforgiveness. Make a list of those who have offended you and write down the offense. Include family and friends, former employers, and even those who are deceased (e.g., "I forgive ___ for his offence of___________"). Set your will to forgive and pray for your offenders. Jesus will never ask you to do anything He will not give you the grace to do. Refuse to give self-pity a place in your heart.

Make sure you have dealt with all painful issues every day before you go to bed. Ephesians 4: 26 says, "Do not let the sun go down on your wrath". When we hold on to inner pain and anger overnight, there is a cementing and sealing of that resentment that makes it much harder to get free from later.

Third – Repent of your bitterness and renounce it. You have given ground to the enemy through unforgiveness, and he has a legal stronghold in your life until the ground is reclaimed for Jesus. James 4: 7 says that after submitting to God (enthroning Him in our hearts), we can resist the Devil.

Three Vital Steps to Freedom From Bitterness

1. Acknowledge that bitterness is sin. Repent of it and renounce it in Jesus' name.
2. Ask the Lord to cleanse your heart from all bitterness with Jesus' blood.
3. Ask God to retake the ground of your heart (where the sin was),

to destroy the enemy's stronghold of bitterness there, and to be enthroned in your heart again as Lord and King.

4. Authoritatively tell any tormentors to leave, such as fear, depression or sickness.

Make a decision at the beginning of every day to forgive others as God has forgiven you. Do not wait until you get into some type of confrontation or emotional turmoil to decide how you will react. At that point, your flesh resists all ideas of forbearance and forgiveness! If you choose every morning to walk in mercy all day, then you will have the grace and strength at the time of a crisis to do so. Do not allow your spirit to be robbed of peace and joy. Live in the grace of forgiveness. You might pray, "Lord, I choose to forgive anyone who will hurt or offend me today. Please help me extend Your mercy and forgiveness".

Remember Jesus' words in Matthew 6: 14–15: "For if you forgive men their trespasses, your heavenly Father will also forgive you. But if you do not forgive men their trespasses, neither will your Father forgive your trespasses".

If you would like to view or download Reuven and Yanit Ross's excellent discipleship materials, please visit their website: www.making-disciples.net. Yanit's latest book, "Fashioned for Glory", is an excellent handbook to accompany this study of the parable of the sower.

About the Author

Jan Whitmore, a disciple of Jesus, is one of God's dedicated and enterprising encouragers. Remarkable in vision, courage and determination, she has travelled extensively in full-time Christian ministry for more than twenty four years, devoting her life to discipleship within the body of Christ.

Experienced, insightful, articulate, and witty as a disciple-maker, she now turns her gifted hand to writing books that stimulate desire for personal and corporate spiritual growth. Jan, a widow, was born in Bath, England, but now lives in the quiet village of Ferring, on the beautiful south coast of England.

Bibliography

Frangipane, Francis. *Holiness, Truth, and the Presence of God,* Potomac, MD: Arrow Publications (1986).

Ross, Reuven and Yanit. *The Lifestyle of the Disciple,* Making Disciples International (2011). www.making-disciples.net

Tverberg, Lois and Spangler, Ann. *Sitting at the feet of Rabbi Jesus* (2009): Zondervan, Grand Rapids, Michigan 49530

Lightning Source UK Ltd.
Milton Keynes UK
UKHW011325061221
395182UK00002B/387